NEW
TESTAMENT
HOSPITALITY

OVERTURES TO BIBLICAL THEOLOGY

Editors

WALTER BRUEGGEMANN, Professor of Old Testament at Eden Theological Seminary, St. Louis, Missouri

JOHN R. DONAHUE, S.J., Professor of New Testament at the Jesuit School of Theology, Berkeley, California

*Partnership
with
Strangers
as Promise
and Mission*

JOHN KOENIG

F FORTRESS PRESS   Philadelphia

Library of Congress Cataloging in Publication Data

Koenig, John, 1938–
    New Testament hospitality.

    (Overtures to biblical theology; 17)
    Bibliography: p.
    Includes index.
    1. Hospitality—Bibical teaching. 2. Bible. N.T.—
Criticism, interpretation, etc. 3. Hospitality—
Religious aspects—Christianity. I. Title. II. Series.
    BS2545.H66K64   1985   241'.4   85–47725
    ISBN 0–8006–1543–3

1732C85   Printed in the United States of America   1–1543

To the Dean and Faculty
of
The General Theological Seminary
My Right Amiable Companions in Christ

Contents

Editor's Foreword

Over 150 years ago Alexis de Tocqueville observed a tendency in the United States toward an individualism "which disposes each citizen to isolate himself from the mass of his fellows and to withdraw into the circle of family and friends" (*Democracy in America* [Garden City, N.Y.: Doubleday, 1969], 506). This tendency stands over against the image of America the melting pot, a land that welcomes the stranger and alien. At different periods of our history rugged individualism and communal concern vie for supremacy. Our present period seems preoccupied with individual autonomy and the prosperity of family and friends.

Christians affirm that they "are no longer strangers and sojourners, but fellow citizens with the saints and members of the household of God" (Eph. 2:19). To be welcomed by God is the Christian's heritage and hope. Under the aegis of "New Testament Hospitality," John Koenig presents a major study of a theme that is pervasive in the New Testament and of significant import for Christian faith and ethics. From an examination of the ministry of Jesus, the missionary practice of Paul, and the structure of the early communities in Luke-Acts, Koenig is able to show that "hospitality" and "partnership with strangers" provide a hermeneutical key to the proclamation of Jesus and to two important moments in the development of the early church's thought and practice.

A welcome by-product of his study are some clear and original insights into such well-known passages as the narratives of the last supper in the Gospels and the discussion of the Lord's Supper in 1 Corinthians 11. He also underscores the significance of lesser-known motifs like the relation of residential church leaders and wandering prophets in Luke-Acts. His exegesis combines traditional historical-critical attention to the development of significant traditions (such as the charge in Matt. 11:19 that Jesus is a glutton, a drunkard, and a friend of tax collectors and sinners) with those more recent methods that uncover the social setting and impact of New Testament statements.

While the book will stand on its own as a contribution to the interpretation of significant parts of the New Testament, it should also foster dialogue in the contemporary church on important human and social issues. Compassion over the fate of the homeless, concern for the presence of the stateless and landless, and acceptance of strangers and those who are different should inform preaching and pastoral practice that claim fidelity to the New Testament. In a previous book (*Jews and Christians in Dialogue: New Testament Foundations* [Philadelphia: Westminster Press, 1979]) John Koenig, Professor of New Testament at General Theological Seminary, has disclosed resources in the New Testament for surmounting barriers between Jews and Christians. His own pastoral experience, vignettes of which appear in the present work, has made him attuned to the fears and divisions within the human heart which cause us to erect defenses against the stranger. Thus, another barrier crossed is that which too often stands between scholarly competence and pastoral sensitivity. The present work is a welcome *Overture* which suggests the need for many new forms of partnership.

JOHN R. DONAHUE, S.J.

Acknowledgments

My special thanks go to students, colleagues, and friends who have helped me sift through the material presented here in courses at Princeton Seminary, St. John's University (Collegeville), and the General Seminary, as well as lecture-discussions at the Chautauqua Institution, the 1983 retreat for world mission workers of the Lutheran Church in America, the Kanuga Conference Center of the Episcopal Church, and numerous parish study groups along the eastern seaboard from Maine to Florida. I am also grateful to my coworkers in the breakfast club for street people at my home parish, St. Peter's, Manhattan, and to the guests who have taught me there. On a sabbatical leave in England I experienced warm hospitality from Dr. William Campbell of the Selly Oak Colleges in Birmingham and the Rev. Billy Watson of St. Peter's College, Oxford, where I delivered lectures, and also from the staff of the Lyttleton Library at Winchester Cathedral, where I began to write these pages.

Encouragements to complete the project came from many quarters, but the ones that stand out in my memory now (perhaps because they occurred during conversations at table) are those from Professors John H. Elliott and C. F. D. Moule; Sr. Marilyn Robinson, O.S.U.; the Rev. Conrad Braaten; the Rev. Richard Cook of the National Farm Workers Ministry; and Dr. Elisabeth Koenig, with whom I share daily bread. The Rev. Vesta Kowalski, who typed the final version of this manuscript, deserves much praise for her accurate work under pressure. Finally, I want to express sincere appreciation to my editors, John R. Donahue, S.J., John A. Hollar, and Therese Boyd; their counsel was never less than wise.

Some readers will recall that the ancient hymn "St. Patrick's Breast-plate" ends with an acclamation praising Christ as the one who comes to meet us "in mouth of friend and stranger." Often that deceptively simple faith statement has proved to be the best description of my life.

J.K.

Advent, 1984
Chelsea Square
New York City

Abbreviations

AB	Anchor Bible
ACNT	Augsburg Commentary on the New Testament
ATR	*Anglican Theological Review*
CBQ	*Catholic Biblical Quarterly*
EKK	Evangelisch-Katholischer Kommentar zum Neuen Testament
ET	*Expository Times*
JBL	*Journal of Biblical Literature*
JSNT	*Journal for the Study of the New Testament*
NTS	*New Testament Studies*
NYT	*New York Times*
par.	parallels
SBL	Society of Biblical Literature
TDNT	*Theological Dictionary of the New Testament*
USQR	*Union Seminary Quarterly Review*

CHAPTER 1

Hospitality, Strangers, and the Love of God

For most of us, hospitality is a word about comfort, security, and refreshment, first of all at the physical level. Thus, if we are caught in the grip of a cold spell, we may imagine ourselves as guests at a pleasant country inn, enjoying a cozy spot next to the fireplace. Or, if hot weather oppresses us, we may conjure up a picture of ourselves on the porch or patio of a neighbor's house, sipping an iced drink in the cool of evening. Usually our images will include other people: family, friends, or kindly strangers who extend just the right amount of welcoming. For hospitality is also a matter of human exchanges that restore the spirit. In addition, the word may suggest a place of rest from our labors and journeys, a place that is not our home but nevertheless enables us to feel at home. On occasion this space, which can be psychic as well as physical, appears where we least expect it, offering us a refuge from real or imagined dangers. Sometimes we apply the adjective "gracious" to the practice of hospitality, meaning that a particular host has acted with unusual generosity and attentiveness. If we are religiously-minded, we perhaps intend our adjective to signify that what happened was literally an occasion of grace in which something more than the goodness of the host was communicated to each participant. Although interpretations of it vary, this mysterious "extra" in hospitality appears to be a widespread cross-cultural phenomenon.

On the other hand, like all the gifts of our common humanity that may serve to ennoble us, hospitality has its shadow side. Some of us will always be deemed unacceptable, unworthy of entry to the place or company we seek. And we in turn will fail to welcome others when we occupy the post of doorkeeper. Indeed, even when welcoming does happen, we sometimes allow it to degenerate into a trading of polite formalities, or worse, a time of mutual abuse on the part of guests and hosts. The ancient psalmist was smarting from a hospitality betrayed when he wrote: "Even my bosom friend in whom I trusted, who ate of my bread, has lifted up his heel against me" (Ps. 41:9). Competition, prejudice, ostracism—all of these occur with regularity in our attempts to be hospitable. Furthermore, particularly in North America and Europe, hospitality has become increasingly a commercial concept. Hotels, motels, and lounges abound; but genuine welcomes are rare. And of course prostitution by both sexes continues to offer itself as a kind of parody of the guest-host relationship.

In the New Testament, where the heights and depths of human nature are displayed, all these dimensions of hospitality find a place. Complementing them, however, is a tradition inherited from the ancient Greek and near-Eastern peoples (and well represented in the Hebrew Bible) concerning a sacred bond between guests and hosts. According to this tradition, which has virtually disappeared from contemporary Western culture, hospitality is seen as one of the pillars of morality upon which the universe stands. When guests or hosts violate their obligations to each other, the whole world shakes and retribution follows. Elaborating upon this tradition, our New Testament witnesses emphasize the presence of God or Christ in ordinary exchanges between human guests and hosts. As a result, the numinous qualities of hospitality referred to above take on an equal significance alongside the moral ones. Readers who come to this study from recent service in soup kitchens, shelters for the homeless, or organizations devoted to helping refugees and aliens will probably bring a special empathy for such blendings of the spiritual and the moral. Many will know from experience what it means to call hospitality holy ground.

Here it may be useful to review some of the actual data about hospitality contained in the New Testament. Some of us will begin by recalling the prominence given in the Synoptic Gospels to Jesus' table ministry among marginal people. "Why," his critics are reported to have asked, "does he eat with tax collectors and sinners?" (Mark 2:16 and par.). Related to this phenomenon are Jesus' parables of the lost sheep and coin, the prodigal son, the great supper, and the good Samaritan, as well as the story of Zaccheus, who experienced a conversion at table with Jesus. Other readers may remember the exhortations of Paul to the Corinthians and Romans in support of inclusiveness at church meals (1 Cor. 11:17–34; Rom. 14:1—15:7). A few of us will think of the apostle's strong stand in Antioch against the practice of separate tables for Jewish and Gentile believers, a stand taken to preserve what he called "the truth of the gospel" (Gal. 2:14). Still other readers will call to mind words of Jesus like the following:

> Come to me, all you who labor and are heavy laden, and I will give you rest (Matt. 11:28). In my Father's house are many rooms; if it were not so, would I have told you that I go to prepare a place for you? (John 14:2). Behold, I stand at the door and knock; if any one hears my voice and opens the door, I will come in to him and eat with him, and he with me (Rev. 3:20).

And surely there will be students of the Bible among readers of this study who can quote the most winsome of all New Testament passages relating to our topic: "Do not neglect to show hospitality to strangers, for thereby some have entertained angels unawares" (Heb. 13:2). With only a little effort then, we can show that significant strands within the New Testament reveal a concern for guest-host relationships involving God, Jesus, and humanity. As our study proceeds, we shall find that the material cited above represents only a small fragment of what the church's earliest witnesses have to say on this theme.

ENTER THE STRANGER

A central part of our discussion below will focus on the biblical view of strangers. Both the author of Hebrews, who drew upon the Genesis account of Abraham's encounter with three mysterious visitors (18:1–21), and Jesus himself, as he is remembered in the Gospels, instruct us that strangers may be God's special envoys to bless or challenge us. According to Matthew and the author of the Fourth Gospel, Jesus once told his disciples: "Those who receive you receive me, and those who receive me receive the One who sent me" (Matt. 10:40, au. trans; cf. par. in John 13:20). Matthew's Gospel also contains the well-known parable in which Jesus portrays himself as Messiah-King on the day of judgment. In this role he commends "the righteous" for having given him food when he was hungry, a drink when he was thirsty, and a welcome when he came to them as a stranger. The righteous express surprise, for they cannot remember doing any of these things. But the king assures them: "Truly I say to you, as you did it to one of the least of these my brethren, you did it to me" (25:35–40). Here strangers are seen as those who give us a chance to show our love for God or Christ by ministering to the needs of others. The following syllogism would seem to be at work: If we love God and God meets us in the stranger, then we shall naturally (and even unconsciously) love the stranger.

Unfortunately, things prove much more difficult in real life. Love for God is a problematical notion in itself, and even when it does occur, perhaps in moments of worship, it does not translate easily into love for strangers. Sin lies at the door of course, above all the besetting sins of narcissism and greed that shape our culture. But having said this, we must also acknowledge that it is quite understandable for us to harbor reservations about strangers these days. For one thing, their numbers are growing. Within our own national boundaries we meet them not only in the homeless and the unemployed but also in refugees and "illegal" aliens. Appealing to popular sentiment, writers for the *Reader's Digest* sound the alert to what they call "Our Immigration Nightmare."[1] Abroad, but not very far abroad in this nuclear age, are the Russians; almost by definition, it seems, they can never be trusted. Close behind these archetypal foreigners in their power to unsettle us come the nations of the Third World, no longer content to suffer their poverty quietly. And finally, there are the "stateless people," the millions who wander about or eke out a marginal existence in border camps or sail the oceans in search of a place to settle down. Strangers of this kind may indeed constitute threats to what we think of as rights, especially our sense of home and our ability to earn a good living.

Some excerpts from a recent newspaper account typify our deep-rooted fears about strangers. After opening up his ranch near Milpitas, California, to a tent encampment for homeless people, Gerhard Siebertz met with a number of hostile responses from his neighbors. In describing the incident, a reporter observed that for these local residents "the arrival of about two dozen homeless people and their six tents [was] both frightening and intolerable." One man, who owned a stable near the camp, complained that the settlers would hurt his business. A teacher remarked that the frequent comings and goings of the campers created "an air of apprehension." A woman in the neighborhood felt that she could not be out in her own streets after dark without a gun. "I feel sorry for those who have a legitimate reason for being out here living in tents," said her friend, "but I also have my three children to think about."[2] Allowing for the probability that some residents of Milpitas overreacted to this situation, most of us would probably feel hesitant about judging them too harshly. The ethicist Thomas Ogletree has rightly called into question romanticist views of the stranger that give insufficient weight to the fact that close encounters with "the other" usually tend to disorient us.[3]

Here, however, we must return to the biblical vision of strangers, that broader vision that counters the risks inherent in hospitality with God's loving embrace of all nations. In this gracious space, the biblical sources tell us, strangers received will enlarge our total well-being rather than diminish it. It is no accident, I think, that the three major festivals of the church—Christmas, Easter, and Pentecost—all have to do with the advent of a divine stranger. In each case the newcomer offers blessings that cannot, at first, be comprehended. The child in the manger, the traveler on the road to Emmaus, and the mighty wind of the Spirit all meet us as mysterious visitors, challenging our belief systems even as they welcome us to new worlds.

In recent years Henri Nouwen and Parker Palmer have given attention to this phenomenon of the stranger, which seems so basic to the Christian faith. Nouwen concentrates primarily on the vocation of the host, without whose active receptivity not even divine visitors are able to confer their blessings. Working with some of the biblical witnesses we have examined, Nouwen shows how ordinary guest-host relationships among humans can take on a sacramental quality:

> When hostility is converted into hospitality then fearful strangers . . . become guests revealing to their hosts the promise they are carrying with them. Then, in fact, the distinction between host and guest proves to be artificial and evaporates in the recognition of the new found unity. Thus the biblical stories help us to realize not just that hospitality is an important virtue, but even more that in the context of hospitality guest

and host can reveal their most precious gifts and bring new life to each other.[4]

Here Nouwen points to the mutuality of giving and receiving in hospitality which emerges when the love of God is allowed to become operative. We shall expand upon this important insight later in our study.

According to Palmer, strangers may assume the role of "spiritual guide" when we find ourselves confused about where God is in our private and public lives. In his view "the stranger is not simply one who needs us. We need the stranger. We need the stranger if we are to know Christ and serve God, in truth and in love."[5] Rather than burdening or threatening us, the stranger comes to teach the deeper lessons of life and to enable ministry. For Palmer, hospitality means

> inviting the stranger into our private space, whether that be the space of our own home or the space of our personal awareness and concern. And when we do so, some important transformations occur. Our private space is suddenly enlarged; no longer tight and cramped and restricted, but open and expansive and free. And our space may also be illumined. . . . Hospitality to the stranger gives us a chance to see our own lives afresh, through different eyes.[6]

Once again, the stranger received is thought to be a bearer of gifts.

The power of this notion began to work on me some years ago when I was serving as a chaplain intern at Grady Memorial Hospital in downtown Atlanta. I offer one incident, adapted from a journal I kept during that period, to help readers understand something of my personal involvement in this study.

> Entering the duty chaplain's office, I found an elderly black man making himself at home. Seated on one of the two chairs next to the desk, he had propped up his feet on the other. As chaplain on call that Friday night, I had hoped to use this office now and then for a private sanctuary, safe from the chaos of the emergency room and trauma wards. But not now, it seemed. The man said he was a minister waiting to perform a wedding in the hospital chapel next door. He explained that neither the bride nor the groom had showed up yet. *Maybe,* I thought. But how could I know if he was telling the truth? Lots of strange folks wandered about here, especially on the weekends. Just two weeks before, in this same office, I had found myself trying to humor an armed man spaced out on drugs. But this person was clearly different, more at ease with himself and with me. We talked, easily from the start, about summer weather and the

imponderables of wedding ceremonies. Gradually I dropped my guard. "By the way," I said, "I'm John Koenig. I don't think I caught your name." "Nice to meet you, John," he responded. "I'm Martin King." There was silence for a moment while part of me turned inside out. I had thought this man was invading my territory. Now I felt more like a guest than a host.

In an instant I had to confront my racial stereotypes and (once again) repent of them. But with this painful self-knowledge came also a feeling of gratitude for the presence of a saintly man and a new sense of commitment to the work he and his son stood for. I continue to be nourished by that meeting.

Some last remarks on the stranger are in order here. Strangers need not differ from us in culture, race, or socioeconomic status. In fact, they most frequently meet us in "our own kind of people," in the families, friends, and neighbors who have become alienated from us for a variety of reasons. It should not surprise us to learn that the strangers who receive most attention in the New Testament are disciples or church members who have suffered unjust exclusion from the fullness of community life or removed themselves by means of unacceptable behavior. In practically every case the insiders of the community are urged to seek out the exiles and welcome them back.

Akin to these strangers but more intimate still are those parts of ourselves with whom we do not feel comfortable or do not even know on a conscious level. Luke reports that when the prodigal son lost all hope of keeping himself alive in the far country, he "came to himself" and remembered the abundance of his father's household (15.17). This turnabout is usually understood as an act of repentance which sets the stage for reconciliation between parent and child. It is that, of course, but at its center lies a positive image from the past that beckons toward the runaway and allows him to see himself as redeemable. Thus, a repressed feature of his psyche is acknowledged and welcomed. The first homecoming of the prodigal son happens in his heart. Our study will show that this merging of hospitality with repentance and reconciliation is a common occurrence in the New Testament.

HOSPITALITY AND PARTNERSHIP

In many of the encounters with strangers recorded by our New Testament witnesses the roles of guest and host tend to reverse themselves or break down altogether. This potential for fluidity is contained within the Greek language itself, for the noun *xenos* denotes simultaneously a guest, a host, or a stranger, while the verb *xenizein* means "receive as a guest" but also "surprise" and hence "present someone or something as strange." Correspondingly, *philoxenia*, the term for hospitality used in the New Testament, refers literally not to a love of strangers per se but to a delight in the whole guest-host relationship, in the mysterious reversals and gains for all parties which may take place.[7] For believers, this delight is fueled by the expectation that God or Christ or the Holy Spirit will play a role in every hospitable transaction. Paul expresses such a hope when he writes to the Romans: "I long to see you that I may impart to you some spiritual gift *(charisma pneumatikon)* to strengthen you, that is, that we may be mutually strengthened by each other's faith, both yours and mine" (Rom. 1:11–12). Here the idea is that everyone will bring gifts to this meeting, but that the content of these treasures and talents may not be known, even to their bearers, until they are exchanged in an atmosphere of hospitality (cf. also 1 Pet. 4:9–10). Often our New Testament writers relate their understanding of hospitality more directly to the outward mission of the church. Abraham Malherbe observes that "a virtually technical vocabulary developed to describe the hospitable reception (compounds of *lambanō* and *dechomai*) and sending on *(propempō)* of those individuals who were spreading the faith."[8] We shall explore this important aspect of hospitality in all three of our exegetical chapters below.

Here we do well to venture a summary hypothesis regarding our topic. I think it can be argued that nearly all the features of hospitality we have distinguished up to this point fall into a category that may be called "partnership with strangers." By using this term I mean to suggest that New Testament hospitality has to do with the establishment of committed relationships between guests and hosts in which unexpected levels of mutual welcoming occur, whether or not the participants are already known to one another. In a sense everyone involved is or can become a stranger. Such a partnership resembles the various covenantal connections that play such an important role in the Bible, except that its terms are more fluid and the element of surprise is more prominent. Furthermore, unlike some covenants, it always tends toward a greater inclusiveness. On the one hand, partnership with strangers signifies a joining of cobelievers, friends, and so on, in the expectation that new forms of reciprocity will take place among them. These in turn lead them to perceive their associates in a different light, perhaps as mediators of God's presence and therefore "strange" in the best sense. On the other hand, partnership with strangers also suggests the forming of alliances with outsiders, foreigners, enemies, and so forth, in the conviction that God's redeeming work always discloses itself along these frontiers as well. In both cases hospitality is expected to stimulate a mutual giving and receiving that will bear fruit for all sides within the plan of God. Even when meetings appear to be accidental or momentary or quite ordinary, the belief is that here too "everything works for good with those who love God" (Rom. 8:28; RSV alternate trans.).

In the New Testament, understandings of partnership overlap to some degree with our modern business terminology. That is, partners may be thought of as people who obligate themselves to one another by means of a contract for the purpose of realizing mutual gain (Luke 5:10).[9] The chief words for this notion in the New Testament are the verb *koinōneō*, the noun *koinōnia*, the adjective *koinōnos*, and their various compounds. Paul, for example, establishes a "partnership in the gospel" with the Philippians (Phil. 1:5) which involves a promise on their part to give him financial aid for his missionary travels. In addition, *koinōnia* can describe an atmosphere of shared worship. Thus Luke notes that members of the young church in Jerusalem "were continuing in the teaching of the apostles and the *koinōnia*, that is, the breaking of bread and the prayers" (Acts 2:42; au. trans.; cf. also 1 John 1:3–7). But this activity too has implications in the material order, for Luke goes on to state that "all who believed were together and had all things in common" (*hapanta ta koina*; Acts 2:44).

In the great majority of passages where the *koinōnia* words appear, the meaning has to do with human participation in a blessing or task or higher reality that is directed by God. Only on rare occasions is the gain realized by human partners considered to be primarily the result of their diligence, friendly sharing, and so on. In other words, the New Testament writers conceive of partnership chiefly as cooperation in a divine project;[10] there is a "given" from God or Christ or the Spirit into which one enters, of which one partakes, with and for which one labors. A few examples will help to illustrate this emphasis. Believers can be partners in spiritual blessings (Rom. 15:27), in the gospel and grace (Phil. 1:5, 7), in mission (Gal. 2:9–10), in service (2 Cor. 8:23), in Christ's sufferings (Phil. 3:10; 1 Pet. 4:13), or in the suffering of others (2 Cor. 1:7; Heb. 10:33). Undergirding and empowering all of this is a "fellowship" with Christ (1 Cor. 1:9; 1 John 1:3, 6), a "communion" of the Holy Spirit (2 Cor. 13:14; Phil. 2:1) into which believers are called by God (1 Cor. 1:9).

But how exactly does this fit with hospitality and with strangers? Inasmuch as partnership is usually understood in the New Testament to be an expanding category, hospitality becomes the fertile ground where it can take root and grow. That is, the mutual strengthening of guests and hosts needs a place and a time to happen. Paul wants to visit the Romans, most of whom he has never met, so that spiritual gifts can be exchanged (Rom. 1:11–12). Moreover, he advises his readers to "take up a share *(koinōnountes)* in the needs of the saints by pursuing hospitality" *(philoxenian*; Rom. 12:13; au. trans.). Here hospitality becomes the means of reaching out to one's brother or sister believers, including those whom one does not yet know, so that new distributions of goods and services will come about under the aegis of God's providence. Especially in Luke-Acts this reaching out extends to all humanity. In summary, we might call hospitality the catalyst for creating and sustaining partnerships in the gospel. Within these partnerships all members, even God as director, will play the role of stranger. Although the *koinōnia* word group occurs mostly in the Pauline and Catholic epistles, we shall see that essentially the same notion of partnership, as it relates to hospitality, comes to expression in the words and acts of Jesus and the writings of Luke. Indeed, it will be argued that Jesus' central proclamation of the kingdom and its subsequent interpretation by the church constitute a key element in New Testament hospitality.

SOME NOTES ON METHOD

By now, most readers will probably have discovered from the table of contents that this is no comprehensive approach to the subject of hospitality in the New Testament. Such works, now somewhat dated, do exist.[11] The direction I have taken is to examine only a portion of the New Testament evidence, and this with an eye toward how that information might reshape our own perceptions and practices. I have carried out my study on the premise that some kind of hermeneutical bond, however slender, already exists between the New Testament witnesses and most of my readers on issues of faith and mission. I see my contribution to be that of clarifying and strengthening this bond from both ends: drawing the New Testament world closer to us where I can, without dishonoring its ancient character, and at the same time smoking us out of our twentieth-century caves, without violating too much of our own historical integrity. To put things all too simply, I want to help establish a relationship of mutual welcoming between us and our apostolic Scriptures.

Why Jesus, Paul, and Luke-Acts? And why not others? To initiate any project with a look at the historical Jesus is risky business, for the methodological problems are awesome. Yet such an undertaking is necessary in a study of hospitality for today's church. For example, it has become a keystone concept in modern theologies of liberation and christologies "from below" that Jesus preferred the company of the poor and oppressed. It seems essential to ask whether this portrayal of Jesus' intentions is accurate and, if so, what his attitude was toward associating with other kinds of people. Again, is it correct to think of Jesus primarily as a homeless wanderer, a mendicant figure like St. Francis? On what or whom was he dependent, and in what ways? In short, how did Jesus give and receive hospitality? And what, if anything, does this tell us about his understanding of God's purposes, or his vision of what humanity is meant to be? Such questions are difficult to answer, but they deserve more than an agnostic shrug of the shoulder if we have any interest at all in the origins of New Testament hospitality. Paul has been included in our triad because he emerges as the chief expositor of partnership in the New Testament, as well as the foremost dispenser of practical advice on resolving inequities between guests and hosts in the church. He alone writes a discourse on the social meaning of the Lord's Supper. When Paul urges the Romans to "welcome one another . . . as Christ has welcomed you" (15:7), he is revealing something close to the heart of his gospel. With Luke, the task is simply to determine why his work contains so much material relating to the theme of hospitality. Only he records the parables of the good Samaritan, the prodigal son, and the rich man and Lazarus. Only his Gospel preserves the stories about a sinful woman who washed Jesus' feet at the home of a

Pharisee, Mary and Martha, Zaccheus, and the two disciples on the road to Emmaus. Furthermore, in his Acts of the Apostles Luke pictures the first church in Jerusalem as a banquet community and documents its expanding mission to the Roman world with a long string of narratives about guests and hosts. In summary, a good case can be made that the combined testimony of Jesus, Paul, and Luke provides a substantial and appropriate cross section for our study of New Testament hospitality.

To be sure, the rest of the New Testament has a great deal to say about our theme as well. In fact, we suffer from an embarrassment of riches when it comes to reflections on the giving and receiving of welcomes in the early church. Especially the Johannine literature, the pastoral epistles, 1 Peter, and Hebrews present us with an abundance of relevant data. I exclude this material with regret (mostly because of limitations on space) but take some comfort in the fact that other interpreters have recently given considerable attention to themes of hospitality in these documents.[12] For the most part, such studies belong to a growing body of scholarship that is concentrated upon the sociological background of the early church's thought and community life. I locate my own investigation within this trend, although I am probably more interested than its mainstream practitioners in beginning and ending with theological issues. In our final chapter, "Frontiers of Hospitality," we shall explore some of these issues. When the whole project is placed side by side with the more strictly sociological approaches, so as to complement them, I think it will be clear that hospitality does indeed form a major substratum in the New Testament, full of promise for the faith and mission of the contemporary church.

NOTES

1. C.T. Rowan and D.M. Mazie, "Our Immigration Nightmare," *Reader's Digest* 22 (January 1983): 87–92.

2. L.P. Romero, "Tent Camp in Milpitas Angers Neighbors," *San Jose Mercury*, 6 Feb. 1983.

3. Thomas W. Ogletree, *Hospitality to the Stranger: Dimensions of Moral Understanding* (Philadelphia: Fortress Press, 1985), 41–43.

4. Henri Nouwen, *Reaching Out: The Three Movements of the Spiritual Life* (New York: Doubleday & Co., 1975), 47.

5. Parker Palmer, *The Company of Strangers: Christians and the Renewal of America's Public Life* (New York: Crossroad, 1981), 65.

6. Ibid., 69.

7. By itself the noun *xenia* already means "hospitality" or "friendly relations," although its only occurrences in the New Testament describe a *place* for hospitality, hence "guest room" (Acts 28:23; Philemon 22). *Philoxenia* is an intensification of the basic noun that stresses the love of or attraction to hospitality (see Rom. 12:13; Heb. 13:2). *Philoxenos*, its adjectival form, has the same connotation (see 1 Tim. 3:2; Titus 1:8; 1 Pet. 4:9).

8. Abraham Malherbe, *Social Aspects of Early Christianity*, 2d ed. (Philadelphia: Fortress Press, 1983), 96. Among the passages cited by Malherbe in this connection are Acts 17:7; 18:27; 20:38; 21:17; 28:2, 7; Rom. 16:2; 1 Cor. 16:6, 11; 2 Cor. 1:16; Titus 3:13; 2 John 10; 3 John 6, 8.

9. The groundbreaking study of partnership as a New Testament concept shaped by the socioeconomic concerns of the Greco-Roman world is J.P. Sampley's *Pauline Partnership in Christ: Christian Community and Commitment in the Light of Roman Law* (Philadelphia: Fortress Press, 1980). My work is much indebted to Sampley's.

10. This point was strongly made by Max Warren in his *Partnership: The Study of an Idea* (London: SCM Press, 1956). In recent years Letty Russell especially has picked it up and elaborated upon it; see *The Future of Partnership* (Philadelphia: Westminster Press, 1979), and *Growth in Partnership* (Philadelphia: Westminster Press, 1981).

11. H. Rusche, *Gastfreundschaft in der Verkündigung des Neuen Testaments und ihr Verhältnis zur Mission* (Münster: Aschendorff, 1959), and J.B. Mathews, "Hospitality and the New Testament Church" (Th.D. diss., Princeton Theological Seminary, 1964). From both of these authors I learned early on to appreciate the close connection between hospitality and mission in the New Testament. For a "state of the art" summary and evaluation of current research into early Christian hospitality, see Malherbe's "House Churches and Their Problems" in his *Social Aspects of Early Christianity*, 60–91. Also useful as an overview of hospitality within the context of the Christian household is J.H. Elliott's *A Home for the Homeless: A Sociological Exegesis of 1 Peter* (Philadelphia: Fortress Press, 1981), 145–150; 165–200. H.-J. Klauck's *Hausgemeinde und Hauskirche im frühen Christentum* (Stuttgart: Verlag Katholisches Bibelwerk, 1981) contains surprisingly few direct references to hospitality.

12. See, e.g., Malherbe, "Hospitality and Inhospitality in the Church," in his *Social Aspects of Early Christianity*, 92–112; R.E. Brown, *The Community of the Beloved Disciple: The Life, Loves, and Hates of an Individual Church in New Testament Times* (New York: Paulist Press, 1979), and *The Epistles of John*, AB 30 (New York: Doubleday & Co., 1982); D.C. Verner, *The Household of God: The Social World of the Pastoral Epistles*, SBL

Dissertation Series 71 (Chico, Calif.: Scholars Press, 1983); Elliott, *Home for the Homeless*; G.W. Buchanan, *To the Hebrews*, AB 36 (Garden City, N.Y.: Doubleday & Co., 1972), esp. 246–68; and R. Jewett, *Letter to Pilgrims: A Commentary on the Epistle to the Hebrews* (New York: Pilgrim Press, 1981).

CHAPTER 2

Sharing the
Feast of the Kingdom
(Jesus)

One of the most significant rediscoveries of late twentieth-century biblical scholarship is the Jewishness of Jesus. Although he sometimes criticized the people and leaders of his nation, it is now clear that Jesus did so from within Judaism and for the sake of Israel. He did not mean to found a new religion. Thus, if we want to understand what Jesus thought and said and did about hospitality, it becomes necessary to examine the qualities of this phenomenon as first-century Jews conceived of it and practiced it. Given the limitations of space, our treatment here must be sketchy and subject to revision in light of the new knowledge being gained almost daily from the fast-moving field of Christian origins.

HOSPITALITY IN
FIRST-CENTURY JUDAISM

Much of the lore about hospitality in ancient Judaism centered around the figure of Abraham, for it was he and Sarah who had welcomed the three heavenly visitors at their tent by the oaks of Mamre and received from them the promise of Isaac's birth (Gen. 18:1–15). This event was commemorated just a few years prior to Jesus' ministry with the erection of a large monument on the supposed site by Herod the Great. For the Jews of Jesus' day Abraham had become a kind of patron saint for hosts. Many stories about his generosity and his eagerness to receive guests were circulated, probably to encourage the development of his special virtue in others.[1] The New Testament contains allusions to Abraham's archetypal role as host in Jesus' saying that many will eat with Abraham, Isaac, and

Jacob at the final coming of the kingdom (Matt. 8:11) and in his parable of Lazarus and the rich man, where heaven is called "Abraham's bosom" (Luke 16:19–31).

Although Jews then as now placed great weight on the holiness of the land of Israel and the uniqueness of their lives within it, they never forgot that their first parents were nomads who had spent all their days on the move as guests and hosts. The grandson of Abraham and Sarah, from whom the twelve tribes took their collective name of Israel, was remembered as a "wandering Aramean" (Deut. 26:5–11). During their wilderness years the Hebrew people came to know this pilgrim existence for themselves and thus grew unusually sensitive to the needs of aliens and strangers who later resided within their borders. Because God was Israel's host (Ps. 39:12; Lev. 25:23), it knew that it must play host to others who were without a home of their own:

> When a stranger sojourns with you in your land, you shall not do him wrong. The stranger who sojourns with you shall be to you as the native among you, and you shall love him as yourself; for you were strangers in the land of Egypt; I am the Lord your God. (Lev. 19:33–34)

Josephus, a number of Jewish intertestamental writers, and many early rabbis drew upon this rich biblical heritage when they praised hospitality as a virtue.[2] Undergirding the great importance attached to openness toward guests was a hope shared by many first-century Jews that God would act as bountiful host at the end of time by entertaining Israel at an endless feast (Amos 9:13–15; Joel 3:18; T. Levi 18:11; 1 Enoch 62:14; Midr. Exod. 25:7–8). In the expansive vision of Isaiah this blessed meal would include "all peoples" (Isa. 25:6–8).

As for the actual practice of hospitality in Jesus' day, it surfaced particularly in three of Judaism's religious institutions: the Sabbath, the synagogue, and the traveling pairs of Palestinian teachers who were claimed by the Pharisees as the shapers of their traditions. From earliest times the Sabbath eve supper was considered a special time for opening one's family to others, especially those thought to be needy.[3] Luke appropriately pictures Jesus as a Sabbath guest at the home of a Pharisee (Luke 14:1). But virtuous Jews were also known to open their houses to the needy on many other occasions (Abot.

1:5; Tos. Ber. 4:8; Ta'an. 20b), which explains why a "woman . . . who was a sinner" (Luke 7:36–38) could have gained access to a Pharisee's meal.

Although we do not yet know too much about the physical structures of first-century synagogues, it is clear that in the Hellenistic world of the Diaspora at least they functioned as houses of hospitality for Gentiles who wished to become proselytes or simply learn more about Judaism (Acts 13:42–52; 14:1; 16:13–15; 17:1–4). Even in Palestine there is no indication that only Jews could enter them. Presumably the Gentile centurion who had donated money for the building of a synagogue in Capernaum (Luke 7:1–10) would be welcome to attend. It appears that at least some of the synagogues in our period were equipped with guest rooms to accommodate overnight visitors.[4]

The traveling "pairs" of first-century Jewish teachers, who included Jesus' contemporaries Hillel and Shammai, reveal another dimension of everyday hospitality in Palestine. These teachers were not rich in material goods—Hillel is said to have worked for a time as a day laborer—but they did have Torah wisdom to offer, and so it was common for them to be invited into the homes of people who wanted to learn. In exchange for food and lodging they taught members of the household and their friends. This practice is reflected in the saying of Jose ben Joezer (c. 175 B.C.E.): "Let thy house be a place of meeting for the wise and dust thyself with the dust of their feet and drink their words with thirst" (Abot. 1:4). In many ways Jesus conformed to this model of the traveling wisdom teacher and was almost certainly invited to share his learning at table (as in Luke 7:36–50; 11:37–52; 14:1–14). It is clear then that hospitality played a major role in the beliefs and practices of first-century Jews.[5]

Still, like all other societies, Palestinian Judaism contained contradictions that violated the spirit of its ideals. Among those who made hospitality more difficult for the average inhabitant of Palestine were the "associates" *(haberim)*, groups of pious Jews who met in their homes to practice the Torah regulations of tithes and purity at meals which had originally pertained only to the temple precincts. In principle, no Jew was excluded from these groups, but in fact many found the temple regulations impossible to enact in everyday life because of their economic situations, social habits, or "unclean" occupations.

Furthermore, a number of people would have simply disagreed with the conviction that temple holiness ought to be reproduced in the home. The net effect of the associations *(haburoth)* was to construct social barriers between themselves and nonmembers. Under certain carefully specified conditions outsiders might be accepted as guests. But an associate could never become the guest of an outsider for fear of ritual pollution.[6]

The degree to which the strictly regulated meals of the associations coincided with the typical practice of first-century Pharisees is uncertain. The writers of our Synoptic Gospels do not mention associations as such, but they treat most Pharisees as if they were *haberim* or at least supporters of their aims. This is probably an oversimplification since Pharisees held widely divergent views on most topics.[7] Still, on the basis of our present evidence, the spectrum of Pharisaic opinion seems closer to that of the associates than to any other group within first-century Judaism.[8] It is probably best to conclude that *some* Pharisees followed the way of the *haberim*. Even the liberal Hillel, a kind of proto-Pharisee, is reputed to have said that no *Am-ha-aretz* (literally: "people of the land," i.e., ordinary citizens who made few efforts to observe the finer points of Torah) could become a *chasid* or saint (Abot. 2:6). This should not be read as a judgment that the *Am-ha-aretz* had no legitimate religion, but it does reveal a distinction between insiders and outsiders which probably manifested itself in forms of social separation.

On the other hand, it is likely that some of the common people, who could or would not practice the rules advocated by associates, nevertheless looked upon these pious Jews with great admiration and used their principles as criteria for evaluating other religious figures, like Jesus (see, e.g., Mark 2:17–22 and Matt. 11:19). Certainly a widespread concern for maintaining basic ritual purity, as in kosher foods, did exist among the common people of Palestine (Acts 10:9–16; 15:19–21; Gal. 2:11–14). We must suppose that this was often combined in their minds with sensitivities about moral purity.[9] It is virtually certain that the stories about Jesus' conflicts with Pharisees recorded in our Synoptic Gospels represent expansions or exaggerations of what really happened.[10] Still, Jesus must have had encounters with Pharisees and/or associates, precisely because they, more than other groups in Judaism, lived among the common people and sought to teach them. As we shall see, some of these encounters produced tensions and disputes.

Jesus seems to have had less contact with the other Jewish parties inhabiting first-century Palestine. The Zealots are a case in point. Although they originated in Galilee, and a number of them must have lived there in hiding, they were not a constant presence in the daily lives of the villagers Jesus knew best. Dedicated to the military overthrow of the Romans in the name of God's absolute rule over the holy land, they would have recoiled from Jesus' teaching on the love of enemies. Moreover, inasmuch as they were trying to build a guerilla force that was both morally and ritually pure, they would have rejected Jesus' patterns of friendship with public sinners.[11]

Apparently Jesus did not meet representatives of the Sadducean priestly families until his final trip to Jerusalem, and then only because he had become a thorn in their sides. Most common people never met them at all, for they associated primarily with their upper class relatives and with the Romans. For them, "the place to work out their religion was the real world of politics, institutions, and the cultic life of the temple (for which they held the main responsibility). The movement was essentially pragmatic, aristocratic, and conservative."[12]

It was to escape the religious rule of such people that other priestly elements separated themselves from the everyday life of Judea and sought refuge at places like Qumran. There, at a safe distance from those whom they called "the sons of darkness," that is, the temple officials and the general population of Palestine which had acquiesced to their authority, these exiles attempted to prepare a way for the Lord by living in cultic purity according to their own strict understanding of the Torah. The Qumran covenanters accepted into their monastic company only those who would subject themselves to a period of probationary testing and gradual affiliation. Jesus probably knew about the practices of these people from John the Baptist,[13] but there is no evidence that he himself lived in their community or carried on a steady dialogue with them.

It can be seen then that first-century Judaism was heir to many noble traditions about hospitality. Often these found their way into practice. On the other hand, a number of forces—socioeconomic, political, and religious—worked to prevent mutual welcomings among the various classes and parties of the land. In diverse ways Palestinian Judaism prior to 70 C.E. suffered from tendencies toward exclusivism. Given this situation, we may now consider a number of Jesus' words and acts as they relate to the theme of hospitality.

THE EXCESSES OF JESUS

The Synoptic Gospels show Jesus challenging exclusivism wherever it was officially sanctioned or accepted as normal. Above all, the challenge is dramatized in stories about Jesus' association at table with the marginal people known as tax collectors and sinners. Such stories include the account of a meal with Levi and his disreputable friends, which follows upon the tax collector's call to discipleship (Mark 2:13–14 and par.); an incident involving a sinful woman who washes Jesus' feet with her hair at a meal held in Jesus' honor by a Pharisee (Luke 7:36–50); Jesus' self-invitation to the home of the notorious chief tax collector Zaccheus (Luke 19:1–10); and Luke's editorial introduction to the parables of the lost sheep, the lost coin, and the prodigal son: "Now the tax collectors and sinners were all drawing near to hear him. And the Pharisees and the scribes murmured, saying, 'This man receives sinners and eats with them' " (Luke 15:1–2). But there is a problem with using these accounts as reliable information about the ministry of the historical Jesus, for as several scholars point out, all the passages cited above must be treated, on literary and form-critical grounds, as idealized stories. That is, in their current form, they come from a postresurrection setting which reflects the young church's own concerns and growing conflicts with Judaism. To some degree, they represent a reading of the church's table ministry back into the life of Jesus.[14]

So the question arises: Did Jesus really associate with morally marginal people in such a way as to offend his contemporaries? There is one odd and very old saying of Jesus that shows that he did. It is a Q passage contained in Matt. 11:16–19 and Luke 7:31–35.

Matthew 11	Luke 7
(16) But to what shall I compare this generation? It is like children sitting in the market places and calling to their playmates,	(31) To what then shall I compare the men of this generation, and what are they like? (32) They are like children sitting in the market place and calling to one another,

(17) "We piped to you, and you did not dance; we wailed, and you did not mourn." (18) For John came neither eating nor drinking, and they say,

"He has a demon"; (19) the Son of man came eating and drinking, and they say, "Behold, a glutton and a drunkard, a friend of tax collectors and sinners!"

"We piped to you, and you did not dance; we wailed, and you did not weep." (33) For John the Baptist has come eating no bread and drinking no wine; and you say, "He has a demon." (34) The Son of man has come eating and drinking; and you say, "Behold, a glutton and a drunkard, a friend of tax collectors and sinners!"

As we can see from the parallel display above, there are significant verbal differences between the English translations of the two Synoptic versions. Even more of these become noticeable in the Greek text. So unless one of our evangelists has given us a total-recall transmission of this material, we are not dealing with a saying of Jesus just as it left his mouth.

Nevertheless, a close look at the passage will establish that parts of it at least provide a reliable picture of events in the life of Jesus and not just golden memories of them recorded by early Christian believers who looked back upon their master's earthly life through the lens of the resurrection. For example, the short parable in Matt. 11:16–17//Luke 7:31–32 and its interpretation in Matt. 11:18–19b//Luke 7:33–34 prompt the reader to include both John the Baptist and Jesus in "this generation." They are the children who call out to their brothers and sisters to join in playing wedding (with Jesus) or funeral (with John).[15] But everywhere else in the Gospels John and Jesus are clearly distinguished from "this generation"; they stand over against it, not within it (see, e.g., Matt. 12:39–45; 22:34–36; Mark 8:12, 38; Luke 11:29–36; 17:25). It is unlikely that believers, looking back on Jesus' life from their postresurrection vantage point, would have introduced an interpretation that, so to speak, "demotes" John and Jesus to the status of colleagues with their Jewish contemporaries. But Jesus himself could well have said this about his kinship with the people of Israel (Mark 1:9; 6:4; 14:25; Matt. 5:35).

Operating on the view that this passage conforms to actual history in portraying Jesus as interpreter of his own parable, we nevertheless have to ask about what relationship the words attributed to him in Matt. 11:18–19b//Luke 7:33–34 bear to their original form. Are there features of the interpretation itself that might come directly from Jesus? Probably so. For one thing, the nature of the complaints lodged against John and Jesus by their contemporaries from within the general population of Galilee (not by Pharisees or other leaders) gives this passage a distinctively pre-Easter quality. According to Matt. 11:18//Luke 7:33, John's asceticism has provoked the reproach that "he has a demon." But we know nothing of this accusation from any other tradition about the Baptist. Nor are we told why anyone would make such a charge. We do know that early believers remembered incidents in which *Jesus* was judged to be possessed by a demon (Mark 3:22 and par.). But this memory makes it all the more surprising that here not Jesus but John earns the denunciation. Such odd bits of data, which run counter to the general flow of the church's memory, suggest that we are dealing with very early material.

As for the objections against Jesus' ministry, they too sound strange in light of the Synoptic tradition as a whole. Nowhere else is Jesus labeled a "glutton and a drunkard." In Mark 2:18–19, to be sure, his disciples are said to be criticized because they do not fast at the traditional times. This complaint almost surely has to do not with the occasions for public fasting prescribed for all Jews in Lev. 16:29, 31; 23:27 (and possibly in Zech. 7:3, 5; 8:19), but with additional fasts which came to be practiced by pious Jews of the intertestamental period as oral interpretations of the Torah grew more authoritative (see Matt. 6:16–17). By implication, Jesus himself fell under the criticism recorded in Mark 2:18–19, for regardless of his own practice, he was held to be responsible for his disciples' behavior. Even so, the whole incident can hardly have added up to the charge that he was a glutton and a drunkard.

In fact, this charge was probably false or exaggerated, as with John, who presumably did not have a demon. But in Jesus' fundamentally comic interpretation of his parable the truth of the accusation becomes irrelevant. The point is that Jesus here caricatures the responses that he and John have gotten from a number of their Galilean contemporaries. Having discerned the spirit of these objections, he expresses it pointedly in a self-insult, thereby taking the wind out of his critics' sails. Perhaps the critics themselves never actually used such a label. We can ascribe this sort of serious play more easily to Jesus himself than to the postresurrection church, where conflicts with Jewish authorities, as opposed to the general population of Galilee, resulted in more technical charges related to false teaching and Torah abuse.[16]

Some scholars, noting that the phrase "glutton and drunkard" harks back to Prov. 23:20 ("Be not among winebibbers or among gluttonous eaters of meat") and Deut. 21:20 ("This our son is stubborn and rebellious, he will not obey our voice; he is a glutton and a drunkard"), have insisted that we should, after all, regard these words as a post-Easter development because of the early church's tendency to "scripturalize" Jesus' ministry in its retelling of the gospel story.[17] But this argument lacks force because here we have no *positive* scriptural fulfillment that could help the church defend itself or render its message more plausible. Indeed, the assertion that Jesus was a glutton and drunkard must have constituted something of an embarrassment for the church since it is never really rebutted. It seems more likely that the historical Jesus applied these scriptural denunciations to himself as a way of one-upping his critics, who also knew the Scriptures. In effect, he was saying: "I know just what you're thinking." Perhaps Jesus overheard complaints that he, as eldest son, had acted irresponsibly by leaving his family (see the evidence for some such judgment in Mark 3:21, 31–35), touring the countryside at leisure with a group of friends who were obviously not trained teachers of Judaism, and depending on others for his livelihood.

Some scholars hold that the title "Son of man" (Matt. 11:19a//Luke 7:34) and the verb "came" (Matt. 11:18, 19a) or "has come" (Luke 7:33–34) demonstrate such a high christological consciousness that we must assume their composition by a post-Easter believer. On such a theory we might well entertain considerable suspicion about the origin of the saying as a whole.[18] But again, this sort of approach proves unnecessarily skeptical. The verb "came"/"has come" need point to nothing more than a prophetic sense of mission, and we know that both Jesus and John possessed at least this. Scholarly discussion about the origin of the Son of man title in the Gospels appears to be permanently inconclusive, but in passages like the one we are examining, where no exalted claim is made, a number of interpreters have come to the conclusion that Jesus probably did refer to himself with the Galilean Aramaic expression *bar nasha,* which is simply another way of saying "I."[19] When we have other evidence for the authenticity of a saying, such as that presented above, we need not pay too much attention to the Son of man debate.

But what shall we make of the phrase "a friend of tax collectors and sinners"? It could be a later church addition designed to show why Jesus was called a glutton and a drunkard. The postresurrection community might have read this missionary practice, which was its own, back into Matt. 11:19//Luke 7:34. And yet, there is alternative evidence that the phrase in question, or at least a form of it, does actually come from the days of Jesus' ministry rather than the period following Easter. In Greek, Matthew's transmission of the saying reads literally: "of toll collectors a friend and of sinners." The word order is unusual (contrast Luke's "a friend of toll collectors and sinners"). Matthew's version looks as if it had once read only "of toll collectors a friend," with "and of sinners" being added later to bring the saying more in line with the Synoptic tradition as a whole.[20] Thus, Matthew's wording could well be an earlier rescension of Q which knew of an objection to Jesus' ministry regarding his companionship with fiscal agents of Herod. These people were shunned by practically all levels of society, not so much because of their ritual impurity or their collaboration with the Romans but because of their dishonest policies, which defrauded rich and poor alike.[21]

The word "friend" in our phrase also calls for investigation. Nowhere else in the New Testament does this word appear as a self-designation on the lips of Jesus or as a charge leveled against him. Nor does it occur as an honorific title conferred on him by others.[22] Once again, therefore, we are probably dealing with very early material that never found its way into the mainstream of the church's stories (contrast the titles shepherd, physician, teacher, master, prophet, Son of man, etc.). Most likely, the phrase "a toll collector's friend" mirrors just the sort of reproach that some of Jesus' Galilean contemporaries would be tempted to hang upon him for choosing a disciple like Levi (Mark 2:13–14). Moreover, the title itself does not explicitly condemn Jesus for *eating* with undesirables. Thus, its wording cannot be derived from the scene presented in Mark 2:15–16 where Pharisees ask Jesus' followers: "Why does he eat with tax collectors and sinners?" In addition, the population of Galilee was known in early rabbinic circles for its lack of interest in ritual purity,[23] so it would not be quick to criticize Jesus' meal practices on the grounds that he and/or his table companions were violating cultic practices, that is, eating with unclean garments or hands, or during times prescribed for fasting. On the other hand, Galileans from practically every class and party probably would find themselves angered by Jesus' regular association, at meals and elsewhere, with people who were known to have caused them injury. For them, Jesus must have come across as a moral offender.

What have we established through our investigation of Matt. 11:16–19b and its Lukan parallel?

1. The Matthean version especially shows us an essentially accurate picture of Jesus telling his critics a parable and then interpreting it for them.

2. In his interpretation Jesus applies to himself and his predecessor John exaggerated versions of charges which he believes to be implicit in the lack of enthusiastic response to his ministry.

3. Behind the charges must lie objections from Jesus' Galilean contemporaries something like these:

> Jesus is a strange kind of prophet or teacher whose message resembles John's. But his life is not at all like John's. His behavior at table strikes us as far too exuberant. Moreover, he invites us to join him, to celebrate something joyful which we neither see nor understand. We have great doubts about whether Jesus is a real messenger of God; for if he were, his demeanor would be more sober, like that of our ancient prophets and our current teachers. But the worst thing of all is that among Jesus' companions are people known to be criminals in our community. It is quite unlikely that all these people have suddenly become respectable citizens. How can Jesus twist morality around like this while claiming to speak the word of God? It's best to keep our distance from him.

4. For his part, Jesus expresses some anger and frustration about Galilee's relative indifference toward his ministry and that of John. But the comic element in this complaint shows that Jesus' attitude is hardly a hateful one that rejects the Jewish people as a whole. Although we are unable now to tell at just what stage of his career this utterance occurred, we may suspect that he had already made a large number of contacts with the common people. His exasperated humor

stems from the fact that the great popular groundswell he was hoping for had not occurred (see Matt. 11:21–23; Luke 10:13–15).

Returning now from these observations to the meal stories with which we began, we are probably justified in concluding that even when the narratives themselves have grown somewhat in the course of their retelling or were constructed in the early church to provide settings for epigrammatic sayings of Jesus (e.g., Mark 2:15–18), none of them really distorts his intention after all. On the contrary, they run true to life when they depict Jesus as a man who drew a strange mixture of individuals to himself. The collective presence of these companions, especially at meals, caused a number of good upstanding people to regard Jesus' ministry as something immoral. For Jesus himself, however, the gatherings of his diverse friends called for joy and feasting, like that at a family reunion. In short, what his critics called excess, he experienced and proclaimed as God's good news.

Can we say more about what he thought he was up to? A number of passages in the Synoptic Gospels suggest that Jesus sought to move his people toward a change of mind and heart consistent with the impending presence of God's kingdom. It can be argued that in Jesus' view this was a repentance from isolation to the fullness of community life which God had always intended for Israel. The change was to be motivated by encounters with God's abundance, offered in Jesus' ministry through the central metaphor of a banquet.

GOD'S ABUNDANCE
FOR RENEWED COMMUNITY

Another early saying attributed to Jesus will help to sharpen our understanding of his ministry. It occurs in the story about fasting alluded to above (Mark 2:18–22 and par.) where a group of people who know about the regular fasting practiced by John the Baptist's disciples and the Pharisees express their surprise to Jesus that his disciples do not fast. Presumably these observers think that since Jesus is some kind of prophet, his followers should be expected to behave more piously than the general public, which usually observed fast days only a few times a year. Jesus' reply counters the question of these observers with one of his own: "Can the wedding guests fast while the bridegroom is with them?" (Mark 2:19).

The term "bridegroom" clearly refers to Jesus. Because it occurs elsewhere in the New Testament as a christological designation (by implication in 2 Cor. 11:2 and Rev. 19:7–8), it could be a postresurrection addition to our saying. However, since the saying as a whole justifies the practice of nonfasting, and since the postresurrection church *did* fast (Matt. 6:17–18; Acts 13:2–3; 14:23; Didache 8:1), most critical interpreters believe that something close to these words actually came from the lips of Jesus.[24] Certainly the picture of feasting with a bridegroom fits well enough with the "glutton and drunkard" label we have just examined. As a witness to the situation of Jesus' followers during his ministry, this passage serves to reinforce our impression that the gatherings around him were essentially celebrations, like those held in connection with a wedding. Whether or not the historical Jesus actually called himself "bridegroom," he seems to have acted as a catalyst for unusual rejoicing.

Can we be more specific about the festive atmosphere that energized the gatherings of Jesus and his followers? A great many sayings of Jesus and one deed in particular combine to suggest that the best name for what was happening would be "God's abundance." For in Jesus' experience God not only provides the material necessities for all people (Matt. 6:25–34//Luke 12:22–31) but now, in a special way, comes near to offer something of incalculable richness called "the kingdom." This kingdom is not spiritual as opposed to physical; indeed the very search for it yields a generous portion of life's basic goods. "Seek God's kingdom, and these things [food, drink, clothing, etc.] shall be yours as well" (Luke 12:31; Matthew's parallel version in 6:33 is less original). Even so, the kingdom takes precedence over everything else.

Jesus can picture the kingdom as a treasure discovered unexpectedly, as the finding of one precious pearl that puts all others in its shadow (Matt. 13:44–45), or as the unexpected forgiveness of a huge debt (Matt. 18:23–35). But it is surely noteworthy that the images of God's kingdom that predominate overwhelmingly in Jesus' teaching are those associated with the production of food and drink or homelike refuge for God's creatures. Thus the kingdom is said to be like seed being sown (Matt. 13:3–9, 24–30), as well as seed growing (Matt. 13:8; Mark 4:26–30) and yielding food (Matt. 13:8; Mark 4:28–30) or shelter (Matt. 13:32); it is like grain being harvested (Matt. 13:30) or fish caught (Matt. 13:47–48); it resembles a wedding feast (Matt. 22:1–14; 25:1–13; Luke calls this a "great banquet" in 14:16–24) or, by humble contrast, the leaven which causes bread to rise (Matt. 13:33). It is analogous to the way a vineyard owner negotiates with his hired laborers (Matt. 20:1–16).

In company with these sayings is another group centered around food, drink, and welcoming where the kingdom, though not specifically mentioned, is certainly implied. This group consists of stories about: faithful servants entering into the "joy" (i.e., feast) of their master (Matt. 25:14–30); the recovery of a lost sheep or coin and the subsequent celebration of this (Luke 15:3–10); a prodigal son returning to an undeserved feast in his father's house (Luke 15:11–32); a good Samaritan binding up the wounds of a Jew and paying an innkeeper to oversee his recovery (Luke 10:30–37); an unjust steward who reduces bills for olive oil and grain so that his master's creditors will offer him hospitality (Luke 16:1–9); a rich man who neglects to feed poor Lazarus at his table and then suffers thirst in Hades while Lazarus finds comfort in Abraham's bosom (Luke 16:19–31); and a wealthy fool who hoards grain and goods to secure his life on earth "for many years" but dies on the very night his storage bins are completed (Luke 12:16–21). Moreover, Jesus refers to his disciples as the salt of the earth (Matt. 5:13), employs the figure of new wine to describe the effects of his ministry (Mark 2:22), compares righteous people with fruitful trees (Matt. 7:16–20; Luke 6:43–45; 13:6–9), discourses on social status in terms of place settings at a meal (Luke 13:28–30; 14:7–11), and promises that generous acts will find their reward in something akin to overflowing measures of grain (Luke 6:37–38).

Finally, in addition to all these sayings, we must consider the feeding of the five thousand, the only miracle attributed to Jesus that occurs in all four Gospels (Mark 6:30–44; Matt. 14:13–21; Luke 9:11–17; John 6:5–13). Whatever else we may make of this perplexing story, we should face the strong evidence that it is probably not just a literary invention growing out of the early church's eucharistic practice. Far more likely is the hypothesis that it represents an embellished account of a real meal which was felt to be extraordinary because large numbers of people participated, because some form of abundance occurred, and because Jesus was seen in the role of host.[25]

It seems clear that Jesus' persistent attention to food, drink, and hospitality is intended to convey something important about the reciprocal relationship between God and human beings. Behind Jesus' imagery is the magnanimous God, who constantly grants far more than humans need or deserve (Matt. 5:43–48). Some people perceive this divine outpouring, offer their thanks to God for it, and act with equivalent generosity toward their sisters and brothers. Others see only scarcity and dog-eat-dog competition, or they turn away from the vision of God's open hand. In so doing, they either misuse God's abundance or become obsessed with false substitutes for it.

Apparently, then, Jesus considered himself and his followers to be a kind of parable of how people live together from God's abundance. As the vanguard of a restored Israel, symbolized by Jesus' core group of twelve disciples,[26] they extend a constant invitation to God's home and plenty. But at the same time they also render a judgment upon all other forms of "laying up treasure." Jesus' movement aims at nothing less than the transformation of human society. Thus it becomes understandable that many people, from virtually every social level, feel the need to dismiss him and his followers as an insignificant fringe group, or to oppose them actively.

But what about the others, the people who did, with varying degrees of commitment, respond to Jesus' ministry? What attracted them to this strange community a-building? And in the case of at least twelve, what enabled them to answer Jesus' direct call, leaving everything to follow him? For those who lived on the margins of society because of their material and/or spiritual poverty, their ritually unclean professions, or their public sins, the answer is clear enough. Jesus' community offered a welcoming place where they could feel honored as children of God apart from the niches they had fallen into at birth or carved out for themselves over the years. There was liberation in this, a giving up of old confinements for friendship with God's compassionate messenger. The joy shared by Jesus and his companions reached out to embrace marginal people, and many of them entered it in the hope that it would displace the sorrows that were dominating their lives. For them, the group surrounding Jesus functioned as a new family where they could "receive a hundredfold . . . houses and brothers and sisters and mothers and children and lands" (Mark 10:30).[27]

A number of Jesus' followers must have come to associate with him and his disciples first of all through the door of healing. For some, this was primarily physical, although here we should note that most of the stories about Jesus' healing ministry preserved in our Synoptic Gospels highlight the restoration of isolated individuals to communities of loved ones. As examples, we may recall those healed of leprosy, demon possession, chronic hemorrhage, paralysis, and epilepsy, not to mention those suffering from illnesses that produced coma or death. Thus, the deeper goal of Jesus' healings was to help people recover the mutuality with friends or families that they had lost. This was especially true in the case of those who required the healing of forgiveness, for worst of all about their guilt was the inevitable wall of separation from loving human contact that it had built. People who longed for forgiveness (or suddenly saw their need for it through encounters with Jesus) recognized that in his community repentance was more like homecoming than breastbeating. They felt themselves invited by the openness of Jesus' gathering and his stories about the lost sheep, the lost coin, or the rebellious son to see themselves, more clearly than ever before, as people within reach of God's abundance.

Jesus directed a number of his words to poor and deprived people (e.g., Matt. 11:5; Luke 6:20–23; 12:22–34), and he spoke on their behalf (Mark 10:21; 12:41–44; Luke 14:13–14; 16:19–31). Moreover, as we have seen, his hospitality to well-known sinners got him into trouble with a number of people in the general population (Matt. 11:16–19; Luke 7:31–34). Nevertheless, it is clear from the constitution of Jesus' core group of disciples and from the descriptions of his other followers retained in our gospel tradition that he fully intended to create a group where all sorts and conditions of people could find a welcome. Among the Twelve was a subgroup of Galilean fishermen; by profession they were honorable enough and not necessarily oppressed by poverty.[28] The toll collector Levi may have been a minor official who lived beyond the fringe of polite society, but there is no evidence that he suffered material deprivation at the time of his call (Mark 2:15–17 and par.). We know little about the socioeconomic status of Simon "the so-called Zealot" (Luke 6:15), except that he was probably not a fugitive or he could not have traveled openly with Jesus. Judas may have nurtured more concrete political hopes than his disciple colleagues.[29] As for the other members of the Twelve, we can say very little about their place in society. Although Luke regards them as "uneducated, common men" (Acts 4:13), it would be unwise to assume that they came from the poorest and most marginal elements in Galilee. One of Jesus' close followers, named the "beloved disciple" in John's Gospel (John 13:23), was acquainted with the high priest (18:15), which may mean that he belonged to the higher levels of society. He was probably not a member of the Twelve,[30] and there is no evidence that he left everything to follow Jesus. In fact, he seems to have had a house and/or family close to Jerusalem (19:27).

But if Jesus' disciples did not necessarily occupy the lowest socioeconomic strata, our Gospel record indicates that he himself regularly criticized the rich for wanting to live from their own abundance (Mark 10:23–31; 12:41–44; Luke 12:13–21). It is unlikely that individuals possessing great material wealth found their way into Jesus' core group of twelve (Mark 10:17–31 and par.). On the other hand, this group itself hardly represented a natural or homogeneous gathering of friends by first-century Jewish standards. Tax collectors and fishermen did not mix easily. In most respects the closest followers of Jesus are well-described by Parker Palmer's phrase "the company of strangers."[31] It would have been a major effort for them to welcome one another.

Interpersonal tensions among Jesus' disciples are reflected in the old tradition that they frequently argued with one another about which of them was the greatest (Mark 9:33–37; 10:35–45; Luke 22:24–27). That the twelve "insiders" wished to practice their own brand of exclusivism is suggested by reports that they reprimanded an exorcist who ministered in Jesus' name but was not of their own crowd (Mark 9:38–41; Luke 9:49–50); tried to keep children away from Jesus (Mark 10:13–16); and wished to limit the number of times they would have to forgive their associates (Matt. 18:21–22). In each case the Gospel tradition, faithful to the aims of Jesus as we have seen them in Matt. 11:16–19, records that he prevented his followers from closing doors on their neighbors. And this he apparently did with characteristically comic proverbs which caught his followers up short (Mark 9:40; 10:15; Matt. 8:22). If Jesus made such responses in public, we can imagine that they themselves functioned as an invitation to potential followers who feared that they were not good enough to approach his community. Jesus' distinctive teaching on the love of enemies (Matt. 5:43–48//Luke 6:27–28, 32–36) fits well into this context, and we must imagine that precisely his closest followers balked at it.

In a film about Jesus made for television some years ago director Franco Zeffirelli conflated several incidents from the Gospel record to capture just this painful aspect of discipleship. The relevant scene takes place in the home of the toll collector Levi, who is celebrating his new devotion to Jesus by hosting a feast in his honor (Luke 5:27–32). But Zeffirelli's Levi looks a good deal like Zaccheus, for he is a very rich man. Peter, who has been a disciple for some time now, knows Levi/Zaccheus to be a notorious sinner against the common people (Luke 19:7) and refuses to join the meal. Sulking outside like the elder son in the parable of the prodigal, he requires a special admonition from Jesus to forgive his brother "seventy times seven" (Matt. 18:22). In this case, artistic license seems to illuminate history.

Within the sociology of first-century Palestine Jesus' core group of twelve would have been hard to classify. It differed obviously enough from the community of the Qumran covenanters, who held that one could be truly religious only by living apart from the "sons of darkness," that is, the vast majority of the Jewish population. Jesus' company was closer in appearance to the learning groups presided over by the Pharisees. And yet a number of the latter seem to have erected certain barriers between themselves and other Jews, whom they held to be invincibly ignorant of Torah or uninterested in its finer points. But Jesus and his followers mixed freely with these *Am-ha-aretz* or "people of the land." While the community surrounding Jesus was not exactly a band of beggars (see below), neither was it a collection of traveling scholars who could expect gracious receptions in the households of the pious. In short, Jesus and his disciples must have confused their Galilean contemporaries. The fact that his entourage worked at all as a group characterized by the giving and receiving of welcomes is noteworthy.

In this connection we must look more closely at the wider circles of the Jesus movement, for without the support of these other followers the core group could not have carried on or grown so quickly into a church after the resurrection. Luke tells us that on one occasion Jesus appointed seventy agents to go out two by two on a mission trip (Luke 10:1–20). This number may be a "scripturalization" of the event based on Num. 11:16–30, but the story seems true to life in depicting a larger company of Jesus' friends and followers who did not always travel with him and/or give up their socioeconomic positions on a permanent basis. The "beloved disciple" could have belonged to such a group. Despite his intimate relationship with Jesus, there is no indication that he adopted the itinerant life of the Twelve prior to the resurrection. In a similar category are the acquaintances of Jesus who offered him hospitality in their houses. According to Luke 10:38–42, Martha used her home, where she lived with her sister Mary, for this purpose. In John 11:1–3 Lazarus, the friend of Jesus who was raised by him from the dead, is identified as the brother of these two women; all three are said to live in Bethany, though not necessarily in the same house. According to Mark 14:3–9, Jesus was anointed by an unnamed woman in the house of Simon the leper, also a resident of Bethany.[32] Peter's house in Capernaum seems to have been the locale for a number of events during Jesus' Galilean ministry. Mark suggests that it served as a kind of headquarters.[33] Finally, there is the anonymous householder in Jerusalem who provided an upper room for Jesus' last supper with the Twelve (Mark 14:12–16).

Another group of followers, who were closer to the core group in their manner of life, consisted of women who sometimes traveled with the Twelve and provided financial support for them (Mark 15:40–41; Luke 8:1–3). The most prominent of these was Mary of Magdala (Mark 15:40, 47; 16:1 and par.; Luke 8:2; John 19:25; 20:1, 11, 16, 18). There is no real evidence that she was considered by her peers to be unusually sinful or poor, though her possession by "seven demons" (Luke 8:2) would certainly have rendered her unclean in the eyes of many. Jesus' group of women followers, whom we should not hesitate to call disciples, must have aroused negative responses from some members of Palestinian society, but these would have been dampened if the women maintained a distinct identity of their own by traveling under the aegis of well-to-do public figures like Johanna, the wife of Herod's steward (Luke 8:3; 24:10). Insofar as the latter availed themselves of Hellenistic precedents—and the atmosphere of Herod's court certainly allowed for this—they enjoyed considerable independence and freedom to move about the countryside. Moreover, they could have extended their privileges (e.g., servants, conveyances, a circle of friends for overnight stays) to their companions.

It is not certain that Jesus' women disciples traveled with him at all times,[34] but a number of them did follow him on his final trip to Jerusalem (Mark 15:40–41 and par.). The most natural settings for these disciples to mix with Jesus and the Twelve would have been those involving teaching and meals. It is possible that the presence of women followers on such occasions gave courage to their sisters from the general population who might have shied away from opportunities for learning or healing because of their restricted positions in society. In any event, stories of bold women who came forward to press their requests and questions on Jesus (Mark 5:25–34; 7:25–30; Matt. 20:20–23; John 4:7–26) or berate him (John 11:21) or honor him with acts of anointing (Mark 14:3–9; Luke 7:36–50; John 12:1–8) form a solid part of the Gospel record. Moreover, Elisabeth Schüssler Fiorenza has provided substantial evidence that Jesus' gatherings were nonpatriarchal in structure,[35] and this itself could have served as an invitation to prospective women followers.

Alongside the women who belonged to Jesus' broader community, "secret" sympathizers like Joseph of Arimathea (Mark 15:42–43 and par.; John 19:38) and Nicodemus (John 3:1–21; 7:45–52; 19:39) are remembered in the tradition. Apparently such people never traveled with Jesus or talked with him publicly, but they may have tried to use their positions of influence to aid him (Luke 23:50–51; John 7:45–52). Two prominent residents of Capernaum, the synagogue ruler Jairus, whose daughter was healed by Jesus (Mark 5:21–24, 35–43), and the unnamed gentile centurion who trusted Jesus' ability to cure his servant by means of a commanding word (Matt. 8:5–13; Luke 7:1–10), may represent a similar category of supporters. Luke cannot be too far off the mark when he notes in Acts 1:15 that "the company of persons" who gathered regularly with the Twelve in Jerusalem during the period between Easter and Pentecost "was in all about a hundred and twenty." Other people more or less allied to Jesus' mission presumably remained in Galilee.

Still another factor that must have drawn people into Jesus' orbit was the peculiar array of economic reevaluations and transactions practiced by his community. The central paradox here is that while Jesus and the Twelve had given up possessions and regular family life, they nevertheless manifested abundance, especially at meals, and invited others to share in it. We must suppose that they could not afford to keep large stores of food on hand as they traveled through the countryside (Mark 2:23–28; 6:37–38); yet their public behavior frequently resembled feasting (Matt. 11:19; Mark 2:19; Luke 14:16–24).[36] Perhaps the best explanation for this apparent contradiction is that people who benefited from the teaching, healing, and community life offered by Jesus and his disciples frequently responded by providing material support for the core group. On occasion, the food and drink donated for meals could have been quite plentiful.

A stylized description of such transactions occurs in the Synoptic accounts of Jesus' sending the Twelve on a mission journey with authority to preach and heal.[37] The Q account of this story, particularly the lean version of it transmitted by Luke, is probably closest to the original and goes as follows:

> And he said to them, "Take nothing for your journey, no staff, nor bag, nor bread, nor money; and do not have two tunics. And whatever house you enter, stay there, and from there depart. And wherever they do not receive you, when you leave that town shake off the dust from your feet as a testimony against them." (Luke 9:3–5)

Presupposed in these instructions is that the disciples were not inherently poverty-stricken. If necessary, it seems, they could have come up with bread, bag, money, two tunics, and so forth, to take along.

Is this presumption historically accurate for the time of Jesus' ministry in Galilee? The financial support rendered by such women as Johanna, Mary Magdalene, Susanna, and others, as well as the use of Peter's house by Jesus and the Twelve, suggest that it is. Thus, the disciples who "left everything" to follow Jesus did so in a way that allowed them to reclaim socioeconomic resources when necessary (Mark 10:29–30). After Easter, for example, "the other apostles and the brothers of the Lord and Cephas [Peter]" traveled on mission trips accompanied by their wives (1 Cor. 9:5). The point of Jesus' saying in Luke 9 is that for this particular mission the disciples are to rely solely upon the material hospitality offered by those who accept their ministry. The first family that responds positively to what they say and do is expected to become their base of operations for as long as they stay in a given region (Mark 6:10; Matt. 10:11; Luke 9:4; 10:7). Paul, writing in the early fifties, remembers this saying of Jesus in another, but essentially similar form: ". . . The Lord commanded that those who proclaim the gospel should get their living from the gospel" (1 Cor. 9:14).

Behind such a teaching lies Jesus' conviction that with the coming near of God's abundance in the kingdom new modes of sharing have become possible, and indeed normative. For Jesus, the network of interdependence that connects God's children must now expand. Precisely in the midst of a partnership with strangers the powers of the kingdom become most evident. James Mackey puts it well when he writes:

> [The table companionship practiced by Jesus] provided an invitation, joyfully accepted, to the good life, an example of generosity from those who felt themselves well-off and, especially when the social, moral, religious or ethnic outcasts were also present, it provided a powerfully effective illustration of the fact that the good things of life, the treasures of life, were equally available to all, and that each was equally acceptable to all.[38]

With God there is more than enough food and home, but this truth must be acted out in its proclamation before people can respond to it with faith. Even small deeds of sharing, like receiving missioners hospitably, can open the hearts of guests and hosts alike to God's abundance. "The one who receives you receives me, and the one who receives me receives the one who sent me" (Matt. 10:40; see also Mark 9:37; Luke 10:16).[39]

Some of those who welcomed Jesus and his followers were relatively well off; some were not. But all found themselves drawn into the flow of generous sharing that distinguished his community. Eventually, to the extent that they allowed themselves to be influenced by the practices of Jesus' core group, the various hosts must have formed economic alliances with one another which crossed ordinary societal lines. Some may have enacted the material meaning of the prayer Jesus taught his disciples: "Forgive us our sins, for we ourselves forgive everyone who is indebted to us" (Luke 11:4). Or they may have followed his instructions on the use of abundance: "When you give a dinner or banquet, do not invite your friends . . . but . . . invite the poor, the maimed, the lame, the blind" (Luke 14:12–13). It is impossible now to locate all the "economic" sayings of Jesus in their original context, but mandates like the following must have been given to guide now the Twelve, now the larger group of followers in their emerging life together:

> Give to everyone who begs from you; and of him who takes away your goods do not ask them again (Luke 6:30; see also Matt. 5:42). Love your enemies, and do good, and lend, expecting nothing in return (Luke 6:35). But when you give alms, do not let your left hand know what your right hand is doing (Matt. 6:3). Forgive, and you will be forgiven; give and it will be given to you; good measure, pressed down, shaken together, running over, will be put into your lap. For the measure you give will be the measure you get back (Luke 6:37–38; see also Mark 4:24; Matt. 7:2b). The good man out of his good treasure brings forth good (Matt. 12:35; Luke 6:45). Where your treasure is, there will your heart be also (Matt. 6:21; Luke 13:34). As you gave . . . food . . . drink . . . welcomed . . . clothed . . . visited . . . one of the least of these my brethren, you did it to me (Matt. 25:31–40). No one can serve two masters; for either he will hate the one and love the other, or he will be devoted to the one and despise the other. You cannot serve God and mammon (Matt. 6:24; Luke 16:13). For what does it profit a man to gain the whole world and forfeit his life? (Mark 8:36 and par.). Everyone to whom much is given, of that one will much be required (Luke 12:48). But woe to you that are rich [and do not share], for you have received your consolation (Luke 6:24).[40]

In these sayings the underlying faith expressed is that God takes an active part in generous relationships between humans, more than covering any "losses" incurred by the one who extends aid. But those who choose the life of greedy accumulation over the life of sharing cut themselves off from God's abundance.

Speaking to both situations is a cryptic aphorism from Jesus which occurs five times in the Synoptic Gospels: "For to him who has will more be given; and from him who has not, even what he has will be taken away" (Mark 4:25; see also Matt. 13:12; 25:29; Luke 18:18; 19:26). The variety of contexts for this saying indicates that originally it circulated independently. If we locate the words within the genre of Jesus' instructions to his sharing community, they make good sense. The person "who has" is someone who receives God's abundance (like a child; see Mark 10:15; Luke 18:17) and draws upon it to deal generously with neighbors. This person will receive "more" for his or her ministry of sharing. The one "who has not" is blind to God's riches and must therefore hide talents/pounds, construct barns to hoard harvests, and, in short, lay up treasures on earth. Those treasures "will be taken away."

Thus, the abundance of God both stimulates and results from the reconciling of a divided society. Within Jesus' sharing community those who shun one another because they feel cheated by their rich neighbors or threatened by the needs of their poor neighbors or simply offended by the moral behavior of others, both rich and poor alike, are brought toward reunion. But this requires changed hearts on all sides. Grasping the treasure of God's abundance is an act of the human center that involves both transformed perceptions and bold choices:

> The kingdom of heaven is like treasure hidden in a field, which a man found and covered up; then in his joy he goes and sells all that he has and buys that field. Again, the kingdom of heaven is like a merchant in search of fine pearls, who, on finding one pearl of great value, went and sold all that he had and bought it. (Matt. 13:44–45)

This finding and selling is the turning away from illusion and coming home to reality that Jesus elsewhere calls repentance (e.g., Mark 1:15). Given what we have learned so far about his world view, it is hardly surprising that Jesus understands even this turnabout as a response to God's banquet invitation (Matt. 11:19; Mark 2:18–22; Luke 14:16–24; 15:17–24). With Jesus as host, the banquet of the kingdom enters its first course. In the little company of strangers surrounding him the abundance of God opens up new possibilities for sharing, and a restored humanity begins to take shape.

THE SUPPER FOR HOSTS TO BE

Jesus went up to Jerusalem to challenge the religious and political center of his nation with the energy of God's abundance. Accompanying him were the Twelve and a number of other followers, including many women. By now their life together had become a fundamental part of his message. Coupled with this message, however, and more fundamental still, was the mysterious personhood of Jesus. Some believed him to be a prophet. Others, sensing that his words and acts raised hopes for a cosmic transformation, began to think of him as messiah king. Jesus' own words about his identity were far from clear. Yet he must have known that his trip to Jerusalem would heighten the expectations of those who longed for the age to come and deepen the suspicions of those who regarded him as a politically dangerous figure. Jesus' cleansing of the temple (Mark 11:15–20 and par.) appears to have galvanized this latter group into a serious plot against him. Its leaders were mostly conservative elements in Palestinian society who feared the possibility of a popular revolt against Rome and/or felt themselves judged by Jesus' behavior. As Passover neared, Jesus must have known that his life was in jeopardy. The fate of his predecessor John the Baptist would surely have weighed upon his memory.

Some scholars doubt that Jesus actually held a specific last supper with his core group of disciples; but this skepticism seems unwarranted.[41] Whether Jesus' meal occurred on the evening of Passover as a regular Seder (Mark 14:22–25 and Synoptic par.), or whether it anticipated the traditional date by twenty-four hours (John 13:1–30; 18:31–40) is a more difficult question which, for our purposes, may remain open.[42] Our primary goal is to determine what Jesus, as the head of a traveling household, wanted to leave with his twelve closest companions. In most respects the Markan description of the last supper (14:22–25) provides us with the best picture we have of what happened.

> (22) And as they were eating, he took bread, and blessed, and broke it, and gave it to them and said, "Take; this is my body." (23) And he took a cup, and when he had given thanks he gave it to them, and they all drank of it. (24) And he said to them, "This is my blood of the covenant, which is poured out for many. (25) Truly, I say to you, I shall not drink again of the fruit of the vine until that day when I drink it new in the kingdom of God."[43]

The oddest verse in this narrative, 14:25, proves to be our best starting point for understanding Jesus' intentions. There are strong grounds for concluding that Jesus really spoke something close to these words at the last supper. For one thing, they presuppose a fast on his part which was not typical of his behavior and would have been remembered. Furthermore, the words are not liturgically useful. It is unlikely that they originated in the development of the church's eucharistic practice because they do not speak of a communion with the disciples or of a postresurrection reunion. (Contrast the parallel version of this saying in Matt. 22:29, where the text reads ". . . when I drink it new *with you* . . . "). Finally, the phrase "in the kingdom of God" coheres with another meal saying of Jesus which is generally taken to be authentic: "Many will come from east and west to sit at table with Abraham, Isaac, and Jacob in the kingdom of heaven" (Matt. 8:11 and, with some variations, Luke 13:28–30). In Mark 14:25 Jesus swears an oath to abstain from wine for the present but to drink it again at a future time when God's kingdom has come in its fullness. This is not necessarily a Passover (contrast the words attributed to Jesus in Luke 22:15–18). Indeed, the closest biblical referent to Mark 14:25 would be Gen. 49:10–12:

> The scepter shall not depart from Judah, nor the ruler's staff from between his feet, until he comes to whom it belongs; and to him shall be the obedience of the peoples. Binding his foal to the vine and his ass's colt to the choice vine, he washes his garments in wine and his vesture in the blood of grapes; his eyes shall be red with wine, and his teeth white with milk [or: his eyes shall be darker than wine, his teeth whiter than milk].

Claus Westermann adopts the second translation of the Hebrew, but he notes at the same time that it is wine consumed that *makes* the eyes dark red, as in Prov. 23:29–30.[44] Here then a messianic king[45] celebrates the beginning of his rule with an almost bacchanalian indulgence in wine. Indeed, he acts like a glutton and a drunkard! If Jesus was alluding to Gen. 49:10–12 with his saying about the wine he would drink in the kingdom, and if (as it seems) his oath originally stood close to the bread and cup words of Mark 14:22–24, which foretell an atoning death,[46] then we have considerable evidence that at this last supper Jesus did think of himself as a messianic ruler to be who would have to sacrifice his life for the establishment of God's kingdom on earth.[47]

When did Jesus expect all of this to take place? Nothing in the Gospels or in Paul's account of the last supper (1 Cor. 11:23–26) gives us a clear answer. Inasmuch as the supper partook of the electric atmosphere surrounding Passover, we may imagine that hopes for an imminent redemption ran high among the disciples.[48] But if Jesus himself believed on that night that the fullness of God's kingdom was just hours or days away, he never said this in so many words. In fact, there are hints that he foresaw an interim period between his death and the final moment when all creation would experience its renewal "in the kingdom of God." One of these of course would be the care he took at this last supper to pass on something like a legacy to his followers. Apparently he did not expect them to be killed.[49]

In the light of our findings Jesus' last supper with his core group of twelve must be seen as a somber feast, at least at its conclusion when the decisive words were spoken. It is doubtful that the disciples comprehended very much of Jesus' prophecy about his fate, for all evidence points to their shock and disillusionment over his death by execution. But certainly his uncharacteristic oath to fast on this night would have alerted them to something awesome on the horizon. Perhaps they anticipated an imminent cosmic battle from which they and Jesus would emerge victorious (see Luke 22:25–38). Whatever their hopes were, they soon evaporated and had to be transformed by Easter.

Where in the last supper is God's abundance, that community-renewing force that had fueled Jesus' entire ministry up to this point? It is present, more substantially than it appears to be, in the oath that Jesus swears. Virtually every version of the Palestinian targum (an Aramaic paraphrase of the Hebrew Scriptures circulating in oral form during the days of Jesus) enlarges upon the picture of plenty sketched by the writer of Gen. 49:10–12. Thus it is said that when the messiah takes up his rule, "his mountains shall be red with his vineyards; his vats shall overflow with wine; his valleys shall be white with grain and with flocks of sheep."[50] It is this abundance, seen prophetically by Jesus, that reaches into the present and empowers him to lay down his life. For only through the narrow door of his own death, he now believes, can God's overflow come into being "for many" (Mark 14:24), that is, for the people of Israel.

But the disciples too have a share in the emergence of this cosmic plenty. Now they are guests of the messiah-designate. As his chosen associates, they receive his body and his "blood of the covenant," first of all to seal their extraordinary friendship with him, to take into their very bodies the peace and trust and hope that they have begun to taste in their table companionship with him.[51] But beyond this, in ways that they do not yet understand, they are also being drawn into the work of continuing Jesus' mission on behalf of Israel. After the resurrection it will become clearer to them that they must take up their master's table ministry and become hosts of the kingdom themselves. And they will see that in this task they must also take up a cross, for the restoring of true community always provokes oppression from those who see it as a threat. It cannot be accidental that Mark makes Jesus' pivotal saying about his service *(diakonēsai)* and death "as a ransom for many" (10:45) into the resolution of a dispute that has been occasioned by the insistence of James and John that they be given places of honor at the coming messianic banquet (10:35–37). Part or all of this scene may be a post-Easter construction, but it in no way contradicts the understanding of discipleship that Jesus conveys at the last supper.[52] When his followers look back on this event, they can see that their participation in his body and blood has conferred upon them the vocation of suffering servant hosts.

THE FEAST OF THE KINGDOM COMING

The kingdom of God did not come with finality in the death of Jesus, or in the dramatic meals of reunion with the disciples at which he revealed himself as the Risen One. Consequently, the early church moved toward conceiving of God's kingdom as a mostly future phenomenon.[53] Nevertheless, it also preserved in the Synoptic tradition a number of sayings by Jesus that confound every attempt to relegate the kingdom to an altogether future time and place. These sayings, which we shall now consider, are taken by the majority of critical scholars to be authentic.

One of them appears in the Q source, in the context of Jesus' words about John the Baptist. Matthew's version is probably closer than Luke's to Jesus' original words: "From the days of John the Baptist until now, the kingdom of heaven has suffered violence and men of violence plunder it"[54] (Matt. 11:12; Luke's parallel version in 16:16 reads ". . . everyone enters it [or better: charges up against it] violently"). Here John is seen as one who helps to inaugurate the kingdom, but in such a way that both it and its messengers become extremely vulnerable. John dies by the executioner's sword and Jesus stands in mortal danger, with the result that the kingdom itself suffers violence. Powerful as it is, it enters into human affairs as a stranger, subject to injury from many of those who are meant to be its guests and hosts.

Even so, God's kingdom makes its own kind of progress, like

leaven raising a lump of dough or a seed growing secretly. It is already "among" those who look for it, though it does not come to their awareness "with observation" (Luke 17:20–21), that is, through the calculation or identification of unfolding stages. The kingdom remains hidden to those who require such "objective" signs. To be sure, it sometimes erupts into public view to overthrow the reigning powers of this age, but always in a way that provokes controversy among the people of God:

> But some of [the people] said, "He casts out demons by Beelzebul, the prince of demons. . . ." But he, knowing their thoughts, said to them, "Every kingdom divided against itself is laid waste, and a divided household falls. And if Satan also is divided against himself, how will his kingdom stand? . . . And if I cast out demons by Beelzebul, by whom do your sons cast them out? Therefore they shall be your judges. But if it is by the finger of God that I cast out demons, then the kingdom of God has come upon you." (Luke 11:15–20)[55]

Given the centrality of Jesus' healing ministry, his "if" in the sentence above cannot be merely hypothetical. This means that for him the kingdom does come in his exorcisms—not finally, not permanently, but nevertheless concretely, so as to challenge the very world views of his Galilean sisters and brothers. The words "come upon you" are best understood as "come toward or up against."[56] A legitimate paraphrase would be: "The kingdom of God has encountered you, like an unexpected visitor." So also we may understand Jesus' pronouncement that "whoever does not receive the kingdom of God like a child [i.e., greet it with childlike wonder, expecting blessings] shall not enter into it" (Mark 10:15; Luke 18:17).

Contrasting the passages just cited with what first-century Judaism had to say about God's kingdom, Sverre Aalen comes to the noteworthy conclusion that for Jesus, the kingdom is not so much the reigning activity of God itself as "a community, a house, an area where the goods of salvation are available and received."[57] Our own look at Jesus' message tends to confirm this hypothesis but requires us in addition to highlight particularly that aspect of the kingdom that Jesus presents with images of food, drink, and home. In other words, the kingdom of God is like a movable feast, a roving banquet hall that seeks the people of Israel as guests and hosts. At this table they may find reconciliation with one another, as well as a true home and a plenty that fills them up and propels them toward sharing relationships with their neighbors.

Jesus never claims that his community is directly equivalent to the kingdom. Nor does he maintain that he himself should be equated with it. And yet he behaves as though the kingdom is being offered through his ministry. In George Herbert's words, he is "such a Light as shows a Feast . . . , such a Strength as makes his guest." By joining Jesus and his followers, especially at meals, one begins to live from the present blessings of the kingdom and offer up one's work to the final restoration of human community which is already underway. Thus guest and host roles become simultaneous.

This double identity wrought by the kingdom comes out beautifully in the one prayer that Jesus is reported to have taught his followers. According to Joachim Jeremias, the earliest version of our Lord's Prayer was something very close to the following:

> Dear Father (Abba)
> Hallowed be thy name,
> Thy kingdom come,
> Our bread for tomorrow give us today,
> And forgive us our debts as we also
>   herewith forgive our debtors,
> And let us not fall into temptation.[58]

Those of us who are familiar with the liturgical use of the Lord's Prayer in Christian churches today will notice that Jeremias's reconstruction is considerably shorter than the largely Matthean version that we employ. Gone is the familiar petition "Thy will be done on earth as it is in heaven," which was probably added by Matthew or his source (Luke 11:2–3 provides evidence for the shorter version). Operating on this hypothesis, we cannot fail to note the hand-in-glove connection that now exists between the prayer for the kingdom's coming and the request for bread. Indeed, this convergence fits precisely with Jesus' message of God's abundance coming near in the kingdom.

From Jeremias's translation of the bread petition we also learn that the word we call "daily" is best rendered with the phrase "for tomorrow." Furthermore, Jeremias and others have offered strong evidence that in the original Aramaic version of the prayer spoken by Jesus "bread for tomorrow" would have meant the bread of God's great feast at the final coming of the kingdom (as in Luke 14:15).[59] But here in his own special prayer Jesus instructs the disciples to pray that this future bread might come now, *today*. Jesus' admonition could mean simply that he wants his followers to cry out for God's immediate intervention, so that the kingdom will arrive in its fullness. But given his view that the kingdom already comes *repeatedly* in his ministry, it is far more likely that here Jesus wishes his disciples to focus on meal settings in the present age as occasions for the kingdom's power.[60] The bread petition thus becomes a request that the kingdom might break through in the disciples' ordinary breaking of bread together. As this happens, they will forgive and be forgiven. Enemies will be loved and goods will be shared. In effect, the Lord's Prayer is an appeal not only for sustenance (both material and spiritual) but also for opportunities to minister. It is *the* prayer for guests and hosts of the kingdom. Speaking it—usually at meals, we may imagine— means taking up Jesus' mission.

Jesus teaches that there will be a final consummation when "many will come from east and west and sit at table with Abraham, Isaac, and Jacob in the kingdom of heaven" (Matt. 8:11). But even now, as his disciples pass through the banquet doors that God opens to them each day, the feast of the kingdom comes. The primary medium for these advents is an actual sharing at table with Jesus and his improbable companions. But this is by no means the only possible "setting in life." All words and acts of welcome that conform to Jesus' ministry both partake of God's abundance and disclose it to others. When this welcoming happens, the boundaries of space and time that obscure God's kingdom melt away. Briefly, imperfectly, but also with great power, heaven and earth intersect and true humanity occurs. If Jesus was right about all this, we are far better equipped for partnership with strangers than we imagine.

NOTES

1. See, e.g., Test. Abr. 1–5, 14; Abot. R. N. 7; Tg. Jer.; Gen. 21:33; Gen. Rab. 43:7, as well as other sources gathered by C. G. Montefiore and M. Loewe, *A Rabbinic Anthology* (Philadelphia: Jewish Publication Society of America, 1963), 281–82, 415. The *First Epistle of Clement,* a Christian writing from the last decade of the first century, also reflects the contempo-

rary Jewish understanding of Abraham as supreme practitioner of hospitality. See chap. X.

2. Tob. 4:16; 5:6; Josephus, *Ant.* 1, 250–51; Gen. Rab. 38:23; Pea. 1:1; Qidd. 39b; Sabb. 127a; Ber. 63b. For other sources see G. Stählin, "Xenos" et. al., *TDNT,* 5:19–20.

3. S. H. Dresner, *The Sabbath* (New York: Burning Bush Press, 1970), 54.

4. See the inscription cited by E. L. Sukenik in *Ancient Synagogues in Palestine and Greece* (London: British Academy/Oxford, 1934), 49, 69–70. Note also Pesah 101a, cited by I. Levy, *The Synagogue: Its History and Function* (London: Valentine Mitchell, 1963), 19–20, 46.

5. For a discussion of the various rabbinic views on whether and to what extent Jews should be receptive to Gentiles, see E. P. Sanders, *Paul and Palestinian Judaism* (Philadelphia: Fortress Press, 1977), 206–12.

6. Jacob Neusner, "Fellowship through Law: The Ancient Havurah," in *Contemporary Judaic Fellowship in Theory and Practice* (New York: KTAV, 1972), 13–30.

7. E. P. Sanders, "Jesus and the Constraint of Law" (review of A. E. Harvey's *Jesus and the Constraints of History*), *JSNT* 17 (1983): 22.

8. Jacob Neusner, "Two Pictures of the Pharisees: Philosophical Circle or Eating Club," *ATR* 64 (1982): 525–38. See also Joachim Jeremias, *Jerusalem at the Time of Jesus,* trans. F. H. and C. H. Cave (Philadelphia: Fortress Press, 1969), 249–59.

9. Sanders, "Jesus and the Constraint of Law," 21–22.

10. See, for example, Arland J. Hultgren, *Jesus and His Adversaries: The Form and Function of the Conflict Stories in the Synoptic Tradition* (Minneapolis: Augsburg Pub. House, 1979), 197–202, and my *Jews and Christians in Dialogue: New Testament Foundations* (Philadelphia: Westminster Press, 1979), 22–25.

11. Martin Hengel, *Was Jesus a Revolutionist?* trans. W. Klassen (Philadelphia: Fortress Press, 1971), 10–35.

12. A. E. Harvey, *Jesus and the Constraints of History* (Philadelphia: Westminster Press, 1982), 41.

13. If our Gospel accounts are accurate in asserting that John baptized by the Jordan River in the Judean wilderness (Matt. 3:16; Mark 1:1–6; Luke 3:1–6; John 1:28), he could well have had visual contact with Kirbet Qumran. John's use of Isa. 40:3, one of Qumran community's favorite texts, makes it likely that he at least knew about the covenanters.

14. For a circumspect examination of these passages, which includes a summary of current scholarly views, see Hultgren, *Jesus and His Adversaries,* 109–11; 161–63; 190–99. See also W. O. Walker, Jr., "Jesus and the Tax Collectors," *JBL* 97 (1978): 221–238.

15. See Eduard Schweizer, *The Good News According to Matthew,* trans. D. E. Green (Atlanta: John Knox Press, 1977), 264; R. H. Gundry, *Matthew:*

A Commentary on His Literary and Theological Art (Grand Rapids: Wm. B. Eerdmans, 1982), 212; Joseph A. Fitzmyer, *The Gospel According to Luke I– IX*, AB 28 (New York: Doubleday & Co., 1981), 678–79. This interpretation presumes that the parable is introduced generally, as in Matt. 13:45 (Schweizer). That is, "this generation" is like the *total picture* of some children wanting to play and others refusing. An alternative interpretation, that "this generation" represents only one group of children, namely those who pipe to John and wail to Jesus but cannot get either one to join them, fails to take seriously the tight a-b-b-a (chiastic) parallelism between "piped/wailed" and "came neither eating and drinking/came eating and drinking." From a literary point of view, the parable and its interpretation are of one piece.

16. Thus it does not follow that if the charge was untrue, the portrait of Jesus in Matt. 11:19–20 is likely to be unhistorical (contra Walker, "Jesus and the Tax Collectors," 226).

17. P. Fiedler, *Jesus und die Sünder* (Frankfurt/Bern: Peter Lang/Herbert Lang, 1976), 139–40.

18. See E. Arens, *The Elthōn Sayings in the Synoptic Tradition: A Historico-Critical Investigation* (Göttingen: Vandenhoeck & Ruprecht, 1976), 240–43. Arens himself, in contrast to some of the interpreters he quotes, thinks that we have the *"ipsissima vox* (not verba)" of Jesus in Matt. 11:18–19.

19. Geza Vermes, *Jesus the Jew* (New York: Macmillan Co., 1973), 182, 260; Norman Perrin, *Rediscovering the Teaching of Jesus* (New York: Harper & Row, 1967), 120; Fitzmyer, *The Gospel According to Luke I–IX,* 681.

20. Fiedler, *Jesus und die Sünder,* 143–44.

21. John R. Donahue, "Tax Collectors and Sinners: An Attempt at Identification," *CBQ* 33 (1971): 39–61.

22. The word "friend" *is* of course applied by Jesus to others (e.g. Matt. 26:50; Luke 12:4; John 11:11; 15:13–15).

23. Vermes, *Jesus the Jew,* 52–57.

24. Hultgren, *Jesus and His Adversaries,* 78–81.

25. J. Roloff, *Das Kerygma und der irdische Jesus* (Göttingen: Vandenhoeck & Ruprecht, 1970), 237–54; Richard Hiers, *Jesus and the Future* (Atlanta: John Knox Press, 1981), 76–77, 143.

26. Sean Freyne and Martin Hengel offer cogent arguments for the historicity of this number within the ministry of Jesus. See Freyne's *The Twelve: Disciples and Apostles* (New York and London: Sheed & Ward, 1968), 23–48; and Martin Hengel's *The Charismatic Leader and His Followers,* trans. J. Greig (New York: Crossroad, 1981), 60, 68, 72.

27. This saying has probably been shaped by Mark to stress the "compensation" received by members of his community who have left or alienated themselves from their biological families to follow Christ. See John R. Donahue, *The Theology and Setting of Discipleship in the Gospel of Mark* (Milwaukee: Marquette Univ. Press, 1983), 37–46. The core of the saying, however, is best understood as pre-Markan material and may reflect a situa-

tion in the ministry of the historical Jesus. On any reading the saying has to do with abundance in communal life.

28. Gerd Theissen's attempt to characterize the Galilean fishermen who became Jesus' disciples as members of an economic underclass rests on shaky evidence. See his *Sociology of Early Palestinian Christianity*, trans. J. Bowden (Philadelphia: Fortress Press, 1978), 34. To be sure, the father of James and John is called a "poor fisherman" in the Gospel of the Nazarenes; but the passage smacks of romanticism. According to Mark 1:20, Zebedee was able to afford help from hired servants. When Theissen maintains that "the fishermen of Lake Tiberias as a class belonged among the 'penniless sailors' who were involved in a rebellion at the beginning of the Jewish war," he overinterprets the relevant text from Josephus. The passage itself (*Life*, 66) reads as follows: "We were anticipated by Jesus, the son of Sapphias, the ringleader . . . of the party of the sailors (*nautai*) and destitute class." This passage does not prove that sailors or fishermen in Galilee *as such* were poor. For a more circumspect evaluation of the Galilean peasant economy in the first century see Sean Freyne, *Galilee from Alexander the Great to Hadrian, 323 B.C.E. to 135 C. E.* (Wilmington and South Bend: Michael Glazier, Inc., and Univ. of Notre Dame Press, 1980), 163–83, and esp. Wilhelm H. Wuellner, *The Meaning of Fishers of Men* (Philadelphia: Westminster Press, 1967), 26–63.

29. Hence the great disillusionment which led to his act of betrayal. See Bertil Gaertner, *Iscariot*, trans. V. I. Gruhn (Philadelphia: Fortress Press, 1971), 19–21.

30. Raymond E. Brown, *The Community of the Beloved Disciple* (New York: Paulist Press, 1979), 33–34.

31. From the title of Palmer's book, *Company of Strangers*.

32. The author of John 11:2 maintains that this woman was Mary, the sister of Lazarus.

33. Mark 1:29–33; 2:1–12; 3:19–20. There is no compelling reason to doubt the historicity of this picture. Luke, who wants to show that Jesus is altogether without a home base, eliminates most of these references. See chap. 4 below.

34. Elisabeth Schüssler Fiorenza argues that women were among the itinerant followers of Jesus who left everything to follow him. See *In Memory of Her: A Feminist Theological Reconstruction of Christian Origins* (New York: Crossroad, 1983), 145–47. The passages cited to support this view (Mark 3:31–35; 10:29; Matt. 10:34–36//Luke 12:51–53) allow for such a discipleship of women but do not establish that it happened during the ministry of Jesus. Before this possibility becomes a probability we would have to know more about what the cultural situation in Galilee would permit with regard to a sexually mixed group of disciples who lived together. Moreover, it would have to be shown how and where the general gospel picture of the Twelve as the only full-time renouncers of possessions and conventional

family life is unhistorical. The Galilean women named in the Gospels as followers of Jesus probably had some material resources of their own since it is stated that they ministered to him (Mark 15:40–41) and his disciples (Luke (8:1–3).

35. Schüssler Fiorenza, *In Memory of Her*, 142–51.

36. Luke 14:16–24 is an embellished version of Jesus' original parable, but even simpler reconstructions of it would indicate a consciousness on Jesus' part that he was presenting his contemporaries with a feast.

37. Hengel, *Charismatic Leader and His Followers*, 73–80, defends the essential historicity of Jesus' sending his disciples out with such authority.

38. J. P. Mackey, *Jesus, the Man and the Myth: A Contemporary Christology* (New York: Paulist Press, 1979), 150.

39. Schweizer, in *Good News According to Matthew*, 253, holds that the saying from which 10:40 is derived probably goes back to Jesus himself.

40. I am not maintaining that any one of these passages represents the very words of the historical Jesus, but rather that their general thrust coheres with Jesus' conviction about God's abundance being the central, joyful stimulus for magnanimous sharing. Nevertheless, it is wise to heed the counsel of Theissen on such passages as these: "Sayings that are stamped by their life-style are . . . far from 'inauthentic'; their itinerant radicalism goes back to Jesus himself. He is authentic. Probably more of his sayings should be 'suspected' of authenticity than modern skeptics like to think." See "Itinerant Radicalism: The Tradition of Jesus Sayings from the Perspective of Sociology of Literature," trans. A. Wire, *Radical Religion* 2 (1975): 87. John Howard Yoder's attempt to order these passages under the rubric of Luke 4:16–21 and thus to understand Jesus' fundamental objective as the establishment of a (final?) jubilee year must be judged unconvincing. See Yoder's *The Politics of Jesus* (Grand Rapids: Wm. B. Eerdmans, 1972), 26–77, and our discussions of Mark 14:25 and Luke 4:16–30 below.

41. Paul, who was called to his apostolic mission just a year or two after Jesus' crucifixion and then visited Peter in Jerusalem not more than three years later (Gal. 1:15–18), would have learned the tradition of the first church regarding the origin of its eucharistic practice. In his own version of the words of institution Paul says that he received them "from the Lord" (1 Cor. 11:23), which probably means from those who were present "on the night when he was betrayed" or those who spoke to them, by analogy with the rabbinic chain of tradition assumed in Abot. 1:1. As for the bread and cup words themselves, the professor of Jewish liturgy Rabbi L. A. Hoffman finds it quite plausible that Jesus uttered them. In his view the matzah and wine of the Passover haggadah had already become symbols of salvation by the first century. "Jesus spoke directly to the Jewish context of his listeners." See "A Symbol of Salvation in the Passover Haggadah," *Worship* 53 (1979): 519–37, esp. 536.

42. A summary of current views on this topic is provided by I. H. Mar-

shall, *Last Supper and Lord's Supper* (Grand Rapids: Wm. B. Eerdmans, 1980).

43. R. Pesch has built the most recent and cogent case for using Mark's account as a basis for reconstructing the actual event. See *Das Abendmahl und Jesu Todesverständnis* (Freiburg: Herder, 1978), 69–103, esp. 85–89.

44. *Genesis*, 3. Teilband, Genesis 37–50 (Neukirchen-Vluyn: Neukirchener Verlag, 1982), 263. The Palestinian targum tries (too hard!) to avoid the impression that the royal figure portrayed in Gen. 49:12 has overdrunk. See *Targum Onkelos on Genesis 49*, trans. and comm. M. Aberbach and B. Grossfeld (Missoula, Mont.: Scholars Press, 1976), 26. But such an understanding of the text must have been common in the first century, for the Septuagint translation of Gen. 49:12a, *charopoi hoi opthalmoi autou apo oinou*, virtually requires it.

45. According to both the Palestinian targum (in all its extant rescensions) and the Qumran scrolls, the figure of Gen. 49:12 is a Davidic messiah-ruler. See H. Ringgren, *The Faith of Qumran*, trans. E. T. Sander (Philadelphia: Fortress Press, 1963), 180–81, plus 1QSb 5:20–28 and The Blessings of Jacob.

46. Pesch, *Das Abendmahl*, 81–83; 90–101. Pesch points out, for example, that the targum on Exod. 24:7–8, to which Jesus' saying about his "blood of the covenant" (Mark 14:24) surely refers, reads: "Moses took the blood and sprinkled it on the altar in order to make atonement for the people. . . ." In the biblical text itself atonement is not mentioned. See 95 and Martin Hengel, *The Atonement: The Origins of the Doctrine in the New Testament*, trans. J. Bowden (Philadelphia: Fortress Press, 1981), 72–73.

47. This means that Jesus believed in some type of resurrection for himself (see Mark 12:26–27 and par.), though not necessarily after three days. The prophecies of this attributed to him in the Synoptic Gospels are probably post-Easter constructions, for the disciples had no expectation that any such thing would happen "on the third day." Moreover, it is important to notice that none of Jesus' prophecies leads to the understanding that his death would simply *produce* the kingdom.

48. Joachim Jeremias, *The Eucharistic Words of Jesus*, 3d ed. of 1960, trans. N. Perrin (New York: Charles Scribner's Sons, 1966), 206.

49. There are other grounds for hypothesizing an interim period. Jeremias has argued that the command to "Do this in remembrance of me" (1 Cor. 11:24, 26; Luke 22:19) is authentic and constitutes a mandate for the disciples to pray that God will remember Jesus, that is, bring about the final coming of the kingdom over which he will reign as messiah. See *Eucharistic Words of Jesus*, 237–55. If this argument stands, the command implies an interim period during which the disciples will be without Jesus. But the many imponderables associated with the evidence cited by Jeremias require us to judge his reconstruction no more than plausible at best. His case would be strengthened if there were better indications that the third after-dinner blessing of the Passover haggadah, in which God is asked to remember (effect) the

coming of the messiah, was in common use during Jesus' day. But even then it would be hard to show that the command originated with Jesus himself *rather than* the early Palestinian church. More substantial evidence for an anticipation on Jesus' part that some years might elapse before the final coming of the kingdom is contained in Mark 9:1, "Truly, I say to you, there are some standing here who will not taste death before they see that the kingdom of God has come with power." See Harvey's persuasive discussion of this and related passages in *Jesus and the Constraints of History*, 87–88.

50. A helpful summary of the targumic evidence is furnished in John Bowker's *The Targums and Rabbinic Literature* (Cambridge: At the University Press, 1969), 278–79, 284.

51. Jeremias, *Eucharistic Words of Jesus*, 204.

52. Hengel, *Atonement*, 73, takes the position that 10:45 is an authentic saying of Jesus originally spoken in the context of the last supper.

53. See, e.g., Acts 1:6; 14:22; 1 Cor. 6:9–10; 15:50; Gal. 5:21; 1 Thess. 2:12; James 2:5.

54. We adopt Perrin's translation from *Rediscovering the Teaching of Jesus*, 74-75.

55. Here Luke's version of the Q saying seems more ancient than that contained in Matt. 12:25–28. See Perrin, *Rediscovering the Teaching of Jesus*, 63–67.

56. C. F. D. Moule, *An Idiom-Book of New Testament Greek* (Cambridge: At the University Press, 1959), 49, and Sverre Aalen, "'Reign' and 'House' in the Kingdom of God in the Gospels," *NTS* 8 (1962): 224–25.

57. Aalen " 'Reign' and 'House' in the Kingdom of God in the Gospels," 223. This conclusion stands against the current scholarly consensus but has much to recommend it. For example, Aalen shows that whereas the kingdom language of Judaism generally points to a theophanic appearance of God's rule, Jesus tends to use spatial metaphors. "One enters [the kingdom], it is like a room in a house, a hall. The meal or feast   stresses the idea of community. This room or house is for men who are in fellowship with God, or with his representative Jesus, and with each other." See 228–29 and 227–32 as a whole.

58. Joachim Jeremias, *The Lord's Prayer*, trans. J. Reumann (Philadelphia: Fortress Press, 1964), 17.

59. Ibid., 23–24. A good discussion (and confirmation) of this argument appears in Geoffrey Wainwright's *Eucharist and Eschatology* (New York and London: Oxford Univ. Press, 1981; original in 1971), 30–34.

60. So Wainwright, *Eucharist and Eschatology,* 34. This is also the position of James Breech, *The Silence of Jesus: The Authentic Voice of the Historical Man* (Philadelphia: Fortress Press, 1983), 51–56. But Breech limits all comings of the kingdom to the arena of human relationships on the ground that Jesus did not share with his contemporaries in the hope for a mythological future. See 32–42. This exegesis seems governed by modern ideologies.

CHAPTER 3

Welcoming One Another
to New Humanity
(Paul)

In the realm of hospitality Paul had much in common with Jesus his Lord. For him as well as Jesus, meals were times of special sanctity during which diverse sorts of people could find their true humanity together in the presence of God. It was central to Paul's gospel that at meals and other social occasions believers should welcome one another as Christ had welcomed them (Rom. 15:7). Indeed, this mutual welcoming was for him the formation of what humans were meant to be within the "home" of Christ's body, the church. Like Jesus, Paul thought of this restored community in terms of a partnership with strangers which carried economic overtones. Charged with the teaching and nurture of many house church congregations, the apostle worked out a large number of concrete directives for the hospitable behavior of his readers. One of these is the only discourse we have in the New Testament on the social meaning of the Lord's Supper. Below we shall explore these and other dimensions of Paul's perspective on New Testament hospitality.

THE GOSPEL AT TABLE

Paul offers his own version of what Jesus proclaimed as the feast of the kingdom. In the life of the apostle, however, this feast was being experienced chiefly through that event which, for him, had begun to transform the very shape of the cosmos, namely, the death and resurrection of Jesus. Consistent with Paul's world view is a ritualized exhortation directed to his Corinthian readers: "For Christ our paschal lamb has been sacrificed. Let us, therefore, celebrate the festival, not with the old leaven, the leaven of malice and evil, but with the unleavened bread of sincerity and truth" (1 Cor. 5:7–8). Here "festival" must refer, metaphorically, to the whole of the new life that believers enjoy in Christ. As in the first Passover, so also here the accent lies upon God's liberating act, which creates a people summoned to enact the divine will. God spreads a feast so as to nurture goodness among humans. "He who supplies seed to the sower and bread for food will supply and multiply your resources and increase the harvest of your righteousness" (2 Cor. 9:10).

But this new life-as-festival is not without practical problems. Sensing that his readers need more than words of encouragement, Paul devotes the better part of three chapters in 1 Corinthians (8, 10, 11) to countering abuses of foods and meals which are threatening the unity of the congregation. In the midst of this instruction he declares that all eating and drinking by Christians must be seen as worship, offered up "to the glory of God" (1 Cor. 10:31). Thus, even the everyday meals shared by believers so profoundly symbolize their new formation in Christ that Paul will not stand for anything that smacks of discrimination at table:

> But when Cephas came to Antioch I opposed him to his face, because he stood condemned. For before certain men came from James, he ate with Gentiles; but when they came he drew back and separated himself, fearing the circumcision party. And with him the rest of the Jews [i.e., Jewish Christians] acted insincerely, so that even Barnabas was carried away by their insincerity. But when I saw that they were not straightforward about the truth of the gospel, I said to Cephas before them all, "If you, though a Jew, live like a Gentile and not like a Jew, how can you compel the Gentiles to live like Jews?" (Gal. 2:11–14)

The controversy narrated here must have been complex. Peter, generally a progressive on the question of Jewish-Gentile relationships in the church (Gal. 2:14; Acts 15:7–11), was obviously willing to compromise on some issues involving the observance of Torah. Nevertheless, after consulting with certain emissaries from the Jerusalem church, he reversed himself on the taboo-laden matter of common meals. It is probable that some of these involved the Lord's Supper, as in 1 Cor. 11:17–34. Angered by what he regarded as Peter's hypocrisy, Paul protested that here the gospel itself was suffering a defeat.

My guess is that we North American Christians cannot read about these ancient polemics without recalling our own sad history of rac-

ism. At the same time, however, we may give thanks for those few
true heirs of the apostle who were brave enough to insist in the fifties
and sixties that the gospel frees us from the myth of "separate but
equal." How appropriate and necessary it was that lunch counters
were chosen as some of the earliest targets for integration.

Consistent with Paul's testimony in Galatians to the common meal
as symbol and medium of the gospel are two vignettes of the apostle's
later ministry transmitted in Acts (27:13–36; 28:16–31). There is
some evidence that Luke, who can hardly be called an objective
historian from a modern point of view, bases these particular accounts
on real events from the life of Paul.[1] But even if this is not so, the
stories show that only two or three decades after his death Paul was
remembered in the church as one for whom meals assumed a central
place in the proclamation of the gospel.

In the first account Luke portrays the apostle's eucharistic breaking
of bread on a ship carrying him to Rome as a prisoner. Driven about
for nearly two weeks by a great storm, most of the crew and pas-
sengers have fallen prey to seasickness and ceased eating. Many are
in despair over their lives. But Paul, who has received a word of
assurance from God in a vision (Acts 27:22–26), declares himself
hopeful. On deck at the dawning of the fifteenth day, he urges his
despondent shipmates to share *(metalabein)* some food with him.
When they fail to respond, he thanks God "in the presence of all,"
breaks a loaf of bread, and begins to eat. "Then," Luke adds, "they
were encouraged and ate some food themselves" (27:36). Paul's
homely act of sanctifying his meal draws the onlookers, who are
mostly nonbelievers, into the sphere of God's gracious providence.
And so they too can begin to hope.

The second vignette shows Paul in Rome, now consigned to house
arrest until his case comes before the magistrates. Luke reports that
he lived under these conditions "two whole years at his own expense
and welcomed all who came to him, preaching the kingdom of God
and teaching about the Lord Jesus quite openly and unhindered"
(28:30–31—the very end of Acts). Here Luke probably wants us to
understand the word "welcomed" as a reference to meals that Paul
shared with his visitors, for the same Greek verb functions this way in
a parallel passage from the Third Gospel (9:11–12). There Luke
records that Jesus "welcomed [the crowds] and spoke to them of the

kingdom of God." Then, toward evening, he multiplied the five loaves and two fish into a meal for more than five thousand. In Paul's case we may imagine that he and "all who came to him" broke bread together as he preached and taught (see Acts 20:7–12). That is, his proclamation took the form of a table talk that encouraged lively give and take with his guests. Thus, from Acts as well as Paul's own letters we begin to get the impression that for the apostle "meal" and "gospel" belong together.

In Romans 14—15 Paul elaborates upon the meaning of meals shared by believers in the face of what he takes to be a serious problem confronting his readers. Recent work on these two chapters by Robert Jewett provides a helpful entree into the nature of the problem and Paul's approach to it. With a number of other contemporary interpreters Jewett understands the Roman situation to be one of conflict between a majority comprised of Gentile believers, most of whom are "liberal" in their practices regarding forbidden (non-kosher?) foods and holy days, and a minority group of Jewish Christians, many of whom have scruples about which foods are right to eat and which days must be regarded as times of fasting.[2] Indeed, there may not be a single Roman congregation at all—Paul never uses the word *ekklesia* with reference to his readers as a whole—but rather a number of small house churches not quite in full communion with one another (see, e.g., Romans 16).[3] Paul agrees in principle with the position of the "strong" or "liberal" factions, but not with their attitude of superiority and their tendency toward exclusiveness. Thus he writes to the majority:

> As for the man who is weak in faith, welcome him, but not for disputes over opinions. . . . Let not him who eats despise him who abstains, and let not him who abstains pass judgment on him who eats; for God has welcomed him. (14:1–3)

Here, as Jewett properly notes, the apostle concedes to his readers of the majority that the other side also bears responsibility for welcoming, even if they, the strong, must initiate the process of reconciliation. The "him" of the last clause cited above probably applies to both sides;[4] it is God's prior welcome that ennobles all potential guests.

In the course of his argument for mutual acceptance by the two groups Paul renders a judgment which, taken in isolation, may seem to refute what we have said up to now about the intensity of his concern for meals shared by believers: "For the kingdom of God is not food and drink but righteousness and peace and joy in the Holy Spirit" (14:17). But the context for this verse shows that Paul intends his statement precisely to *highlight* the significance of meals in the church. Because of disputes about food and drink among Roman believers there have been few common meals and, we must therefore surmise, few if any gatherings of the whole community for the Lord's Supper. In Paul's view this kind of separation prevents exactly that mutuality between Jews and Gentiles (or by analogy, between any racial or social groups in conflict) that the gospel most strenuously urges. Thus the passage means that Paul's readers, on both sides, must become more tolerant of one another's meal practices, thereby creating more opportunities for sharing the gifts of the Spirit *at table*. And this must be done without forcing any participants to act against their conscience (14:19–23). The so-called "strong" are to "bear with the failings of the weak, and not to please [themselves]" (15:1). That is, believers whose conscience will allow for a flexible meal practice must be the first to modify their behavior in order to bring all factions together.

The climax to Paul's argument, written primarily to Gentiles, but clearly with some Jewish Christians in mind as well (see 2:17—4:24), occurs in Rom. 15:7–10.

> (7) Welcome one another, therefore, as Christ has welcomed you, for the glory of God. (8) For I tell you that Christ became a servant to the circumcised to show God's truthfulness, in order to confirm the promises given to the patriarchs, (9) and in order that the Gentiles might glorify God for his mercy. As it is written, "Therefore I will praise thee among the Gentiles, and sing to thy name"; (10) and again it is said, "Rejoice, O Gentiles, with his people."

In context, this welcoming is surely to be understood as something that takes place first of all at table. Indeed, when Paul refers to Christ as "a servant *(diakonos)* to the circumcised," he may well be recalling the Lord's table ministry for Israel's renewal.

The scriptural citation from 2 Sam. 22:50 which Paul employs in 15:9 ("I will praise thee among the Gentiles") is best understood as an aside to Jewish believers. Then, in 15:10 the apostle turns back to his Gentile readers. Both groups at Rome are to praise God "among" or "with" the other; for it is God's will, unfolding on earth in the progress of the gospel, that all nations join together in worshiping their Creator. In summary, Paul's argument functions to convince his Roman readers that their meal practices, displayed before the world in the imperial capital, should serve as windows into God's cosmic plan. Everyday welcomings of the "other," especially at table, are really acts of worship "for the glory of God" (15:7). Indeed, Paul seems to be hinting that these little breaches in the walls that isolate various members of the human family from one another will actually speed the final coming of God's kingdom (see the unexpected shift from language about praise in 15:11 to a prophecy of Jesus' return in 15:12, which suggests that Paul linked the two in a causal relationship).

COMING HOME TO NEW HUMANITY

The hortatory tone of Paul's letters makes it clear that in his view the communities to which he writes have a great deal of growing up to do. For him, life in the church is always a matter of becoming as well as being. Nevertheless, one dare not underestimate the being. Something transformative has happened to those who believe and are baptized. They have found themselves drawn into a new form of life where there is "neither Jew nor Greek, . . . neither slave nor free, . . . neither male nor female" (Gal. 3:28). Out of diverse individuals one organism is being formed. Yet this is a corporate life that does not destroy the identities of its members but honors them, more than they have ever been honored before, as receivers and givers of divine gifts (1 Corinthians 12—14).[5]

It is consistent with Paul's vision to think of the new humanity, which is being shaped in Christ's body according to his image (2 Cor. 3:18), as a home. In Christ, the apostle holds, people may feel most at peace with themselves, most free to take up their share in God's saving plan for the world. Baptism is the believer's first welcome into his or her community home. At this festive entrance, everyone dons a new garment, according to the customs of Middle Eastern hospitality: "For as many of you as were baptized into Christ have put on Christ" (Gal. 3:27). The spatial metaphors here are revealing. One is in Christ not only as a body but also as a cloak, and these familiar enclosures are fashioned by the Lord *from other people.* Through the living ties of the Spirit they become not hell (as Jean-Paul Sartre maintained in his play *No Exit*) but home.

One of Paul's Jewish Christian disciples, the author of Ephesians, enlarges this vision of the new humanity to even more mystical proportions. After showing how Christ brings aliens and strangers into the commonwealth of Israel so as to "create in himself one new man [person]," he concludes:

> (17) And he came and preached peace to you who were far off and peace to those who were near; (18) for through him we both have one access in one Spirit to the Father. (19) So then you are no longer strangers and sojourners, but you are fellow citizens with the saints and members of the household of God, (20) built on the foundation of the apostles and prophets, Christ Jesus himself being the cornerstone, (21) in whom the whole structure is joined together and grows into a holy temple in the Lord; (22) in whom you also are built into it for a dwelling place of God in the Spirit. (Eph. 2:17–22)

Here spatial metaphors intermingle in a way that both confuses and enriches us. For example, the Greek word for "access" in v. 18 literally means "entranceway to a hall." So Christ, through the Spirit, provides a living welcome to the presence of God (see Rom. 5:1–2). But he himself is also the cornerstone of the hall into which believers are fitted like stones. At the same time this cornerstone or front doorway somehow encloses the whole house (v. 21) and joins the pieces together like mortar. Moreover, the house grows, so we are not to think of ordinary stone but of something organic. This living structure then becomes a "dwelling place of God in the Spirit."

Perhaps our author experienced these figures as visions that changed like the patterns of a kaleidoscope even as he contemplated them. In any event, the point that relates to our inquiry comes through clearly enough. Christ labors to build a new temple for God—out of people. He surrounds his people, inhabits them, nurtures them. They, the new humanity, are their own home-in-process as they grow toward that day when God will be altogether in their midst (*panta en pasin*, as the apostle puts it in 1 Cor. 15:28). Until this consummation it may be said that God's home too remains incomplete. When St. Augustine concluded that our hearts would search and long until they found their rest in God, he was expressing only one side of our guest-host relationship with our Creator.

Paul himself refers to Christ's church as "the household of faith" (Gal. 6:10) and the "building" or "temple" of God (1 Cor. 3:9–17; 6:19–20). In 1 Cor. 14:4, 17 he uses the verb *oikodomein* ("build up a dwelling") to describe what believers do for one another in giving and receiving their spiritual gifts. No wonder it became absolutely paramount for the apostle to lay stress on everyday hospitality. If God's own dwelling is being built on earth through gift exchanges among humans, then the visiting of one's sisters and brothers for the purpose of a mutual, charismatic strengthening turns out to be not just a courtesy but the very work of the gospel (Rom. 1:11–12). Even the greetings sent by one group of believers to another become a form of gospel enactment, especially when they are accompanied by short stories of how people have served and cared for one another (Romans 16; 1 Corinthians 16; Phil. 2:19–20; 4:14–23; Col. 4:17–18; Philemon).

Fundamental to the new humanity in Christ, the house of God a-building, is a fluid tension between unity and equality among believers. Unity comes first in Paul's mind because for him an ongoing society among the diverse people who are being conformed to God's new prototype person (Rom. 8:15–17, 29; 1 Cor. 10:16–17; 15:23, 42–50; Gal. 4:1–6) is the only reliable foundation for achieving equity.[6] Thus, the apostle does not anticipate that all socioeconomic differences will simply disappear when people enter the body of Christ. The enthusiastic baptismal confession that slavery, racism, and sexual dominance have passed away (Gal. 3:28a) is a truth seen through God's eyes and can be realized only in part within the structures of the "present evil age" (Gal. 1:4). Moreover, this progress itself always derives from a prior unity: "for you are all one in Christ Jesus" (Gal. 3:28b). Nevertheless, unity in Christ inevitably produces measurable socioeconomic changes in the community life of believers. For Paul, the gospel requires that we see God, and therefore ourselves, as God's dwelling place, actively at work in reversing the conventional hierarchies of this age:

> For consider your call, brethren; not many of you were wise according to worldly standards, not many were powerful, not many were of noble birth; but God chose what is foolish in the world to shame the strong, God chose what is low and despised in the world, even things that are

not, to bring to nothing things that are, so that no human being might
boast in the presence of God. (1 Cor. 1:26–29)

While holding on to this conviction, Paul simultaneously portrays
agapē love as the great leveler within Christ's body. Differences in
gifts, talents, and socioeconomic positions will continue to exist
among believers regardless of the hierarchical reversals that take
place. But through love the benefits of these diverse "goods" can be
so distributed, beginning in worship, that all members receive due
honor and strengthening for their particular vocations (see esp. 1 Cor.
12—14; 7:17–24).

New social relationships were actually achieved in the Pauline
churches. Moreover, they became visible enough to pagan neighbors
to cause offense, sometimes because common decency was thought to
be violated (1 Cor. 5:1–2), and sometimes because traditional as-
sumptions about family structures, such as the subordination of wives
to husbands, were seen to be challenged (1 Corinthians 11, 14). On
the other hand, many outsiders must have felt a strong attraction to
the novelties practiced by Christians. We know, for example, that
curious visitors attended the worship meetings of the Corinthian
church and that Paul expected them to sense God's presence there (1
Cor. 14:16, 23). Particularly among the growing numbers of marginal
people in first-century society, for example, independent women,
Jews, and freed slaves who possessed a certain amount of wealth but,
for reasons of pedigree, were stigmatized by the patricians of the
empire, "the intimacy of the Christian groups" would have been perceived as a "welcome refuge" from a cruel world.[7]

By their very nature the Pauline communities exhibited what
Wayne Meeks has termed "social contradictions."[8] Among these was
a type of leadership that could be exercised by people of high or low
estate, though in either case with the typical result that all members
felt empowered by the Spirit to play more authentic roles than those
assigned to them by imperial society. And yet these public roles were
not necessarily renounced, because new gifts and tasks from God
could be found precisely within them. "For he who was called in the
Lord as a slave is a freedman of the Lord. Likewise he who was freed
when called is a slave of Christ" (1 Cor. 7:22). In short, it is appropriate to conclude with Meeks that these "odd little groups [of believers]

in a dozen or so cities of the Roman East were engaged, though they would not have put it quite this way, in constructing a new world."[9] Perhaps the communities themselves would have said that through the Spirit they were building up God's new house in their midst, a house that would someday include all nations.

We catch a modern glimpse of this building process in a scene from Alan Paton's historical novel, *Ah, But Your Land Is Beautiful*. There Paton tells a story from the early days of post-World War II apartheid in South Africa when the emerging laws could still be tested. An Afrikaner judge, responding to the urgent invitation of a black pastor, visits the latter's church on Maundy Thursday to show the parishioners that not all whites have turned against them. Simply by worshiping in this church the judge risks his career. But the pastor, who perhaps knows the judge's integrity better than he himself does, has made a further request, namely, that he join with members of the congregation in a foot-washing service. The feet presented to him are those of a woman who has worked as a servant in his house for more than thirty years. Some of the worshipers gasp as Jan Christiaan Olivier kneels before Martha Fortuin. The story concludes: "Then he took both her feet in his hands with gentleness, for they were no doubt tired with much serving, and he kissed them both. Then Martha Fortuin and many others in the Holy Church of Zion fell a-weeping."[10] Novelist Paton adds that this incident was picked up by some of the leading English and American newspapers and that Judge Olivier's career was indeed curtailed. One wonders, though, whether the South Africa of today would not be considerably different if such exchanges between black and white Christians had occurred on a broad scale in the 1950s.

HOUSE CHURCH HOSPITALITY

It is consistent with Paul's theology of the cross that he saw God's renewal of the cosmos taking place most publicly among gatherings of ten to forty people in quite ordinary family dwellings.[11] Given his convictions about the imminent end of the present age, the apostle probably envisioned no grander setting in the future for the earthly life of the church. This means that his thoughts about mission and leadership, and even such exalted concepts as "salvation," were worked out in this humble environment and designed explicitly for it.

As a frequent traveler Paul felt special affection for the small house church communities he had founded and/or visited. Some were like home bases to him. The apostle had probably been baptized and welcomed at table in the Damascus house church to which Ananias belonged (Acts 9:18–19). Later, at Antioch, Paul functioned as a prophet-teacher in a church that split into at least two house groups over the issue of whether Jewish believers could eat meals with their Gentile counterparts (Acts 13:1–3; Gal. 2:11–15). Luke reports that in Ephesus, where such divisions seem not to have taken place, Paul taught "from house to house" (Acts 20:20), probably because he placed high value on the intimacy and informality of small groups. The apostle's letters assume multiple house communities within some urban churches (Romans 14—16; 1 Corinthians 1, 11; Col. 4:15), and although this configuration proved vulnerable to cliquishness and exclusivism, the apostle never challenged it as such or set forth an alternative. He must have thought that the desirability of household groups, especially for exchanging spiritual gifts (Rom. 1:11–12; cf. also 1 Pet. 4:9–11), far outweighed their dangers. Thus he provides no directives for disbanding the Corinthian or Roman factions. Rather, he urges all groups to welcome one another.

The Pauline house churches must have derived their organization, such as it was, primarily from Hellenistic synagogues and the extended family structures of Greco-Roman households.[12] In addition, they probably borrowed practices from craft guilds or other associations formed by special interest groups.[13] But for Paul it was no less than the Holy Spirit who continued to weave these various threads into new partnerships, where the grace of Jesus Christ and the love of God abounded (2 Cor. 13:14). The social boundaries that separated these house church communities from the outside world would have been relatively porous. Both synagogues and households expected visitors; people did not think of them as essentially secret places. Nobles and slaves, rich and poor mixed together in them. And in the church this interaction would take on a peculiar shape, for the etiquette of the Spirit was always breaking the teacups of polite convention, choosing "what is low and despised in the world . . . so that no human being might boast in the presence of God" (1 Cor. 1:28–29).

Although baptism marked one's entry into the body of Christ and thus provided a clear distinction between insiders and outsiders, the

Lord's risen body was thought by Paul to have heavenly dimensions and to be battling unseen powers of evil at every level of the cosmic hierarchy (1 Cor. 15:20–25). As a consequence, the work of Christ's life-giving Spirit (15:45) had to extend beyond the measurable boundaries of the house church. Engaged with their Lord in a world-transforming movement, believers would have thought it natural to carry on public commerce with their neighbors (e.g., the Corinthian Christians who ate with their pagan friends; 1 Corinthians 8—10). Like the synagogues, Pauline churches opened at least some of their worship services to outsiders (1 Cor. 14:16–25). It is uncertain whether these included celebrations of the Lord's Supper, although the numinous quality ascribed to the eucharistic elements by Paul and his readers (1 Corinthians 10—11) suggests that nonbelievers could not have partaken of them even if they were present as visitors. In any case the earliest indication that Christian meals were viewed by outsiders as secret events is Pliny's letter to Trajan, usually dated between 110–114 C.E.[14] But by this time the church had gone partially underground to escape persecution from the state. During the Pauline period, that is, up to the persecution under Nero in 64 C.E., most pagans who knew about house churches would probably have viewed them as hospitable institutions, rather like synagogues but more radical in their claims.

Much of the welcoming associated with house churches could be experienced only on the inside. To the degree that small Christian groups lived up to the models provided for them in Paul's epistles, visitors would notice a great deal of mutual touching among believers. This included the physical contact of laying on hands in connection with baptisms, commissionings to various ministries, and healings. Especially the last must have proved a significant point of encounter between house churches and their neighbors. The "holy kiss," probably a kind of embrace, was also a trademark of the Christian communities (1 Thess. 5:26; 1 Cor. 16:20; Rom. 16:16), although the practice was not unique with believers.[15] Moreover, a certain sharing of material possessions must have occurred among church members, for while Paul does not advocate the common ownership of property, he frequently holds up the ideal of generosity to his readers (Rom. 12:8, 13; 1 Cor. 16:2; 2 Corinthians 8—9; Gal. 6:6–10; Phil. 4:10–22).

But another form of touching was also much in evidence among believers in house church settings. This was the touching of one another's spirits, no less real to early Christians than ministrations to their bodies. Such contact happened in corporate prayers, tongues, teachings, songs ("... be filled with the Spirit, addressing one another in psalms and hymns and spiritual songs ... ", Eph. 5:19; see also Col. 3:16; 1 Cor. 14:26), and preeminently, according to Paul, in prophecies directed to the whole congregation at worship (1 Corinthians 14). According to the apostle, prophecy was the highest *charisma* (1 Cor. 14:1; Rom. 12:6), for in it God had provided the most direct public way of communicating encouragements, admonitions, judgments, and present-future visions (1 Corinthians 14, esp. vv. 1–5). Words of prophecy were not considered to be ordinary words but sayings from on high that went straight to the hearts of their hearers. Indeed, visitors who witnessed this gift in action among church members might well experience it as a message from God intended specifically for them:

> If all prophesy, and an unbeliever or outsider enters, he is convicted by all, he is called to account by all, the secrets of his heart are disclosed; and so, falling on his face, he will worship God and declare that God is really among you. (1 Cor. 14:24–25)

The last clause in this passage is an allusion to two Old Testament texts (Isa. 45:12–14 and Zech. 8:14–23) which show Gentiles being led to confess God's presence through the contemplation of divine blessings showered upon the Jewish people. This means that what Paul describes in the Corinthian church is not a reading of the visitor's mind but a disclosure to this person through the verbal interaction among members of the congregation. The visitor feels drawn into what is happening, awakened by the truth and goodness of it to his or her authentic self. Thus the regular prophesying of Christians to one another becomes a powerful invitation to outsiders to join the body of Christ.

In examining house church hospitality we should, by way of conclusion, give some attention to the houses themselves, and to their owners. As we noted above, provincial Greco-Roman homes would ordinarily contain room for no more than forty people in their largest hall or atrium.[16] This would be the customary space in which the "whole church" assembled for such events as the Lord's Supper and the general sharing of spiritual gifts (1 Cor. 11:20, 33; 14:23; Rom. 16:23). At other times smaller meetings might take place in more modest dwellings. Here an obvious point must be made: somebody had to provide the physical surroundings necessary for church activities, and those donors were clearly people well off enough to own or rent the dwellings.

Names of people who fit this description appear with some regularity in the Pauline corpus: Gaius of Corinth, who was host to Paul and the whole church (Rom. 16:23); Philemon the slave owner, who enjoyed a reputation for refreshing the saints at the church in his house (Philemon 2–7) and who was asked to provide a guest room for Paul (22); Aquila and Priscilla, the tentmakers with whom Paul stayed during his first visit to Corinth (Acts 18:1–3), who later hosted a church in Ephesus (1 Cor. 16:19), and then, having returned to their original home in Rome, placed this facility too at the disposal of a Christian group (Rom. 16:3–5); Chloe, whose household in Corinth contained believers (1 Cor. 1:11); Nympha, in whose home a portion of the Laodicean church met (Col. 4:15); and the household of Stephanas, also in Corinth, whose members "devoted themselves to the service *(diakonia)* of the saints" (1 Cor. 16:15). Stephanas, we learn from 1 Cor. 16:17, possessed sufficient funds to make a personal visit to Paul in Ephesus.

These Christians of means must have exercised some degree of leadership in the churches they hosted—Paul recommends that the Corinthians subject themselves to people like Stephanas (1 Cor 16:16)—and yet it is not at all clear that, as a group, they comprised the prophets and teachers who ranked just behind apostles in the everyday spiritual direction of the church (1 Cor. 12:28). Priscilla and Aquila certainly were spiritual leaders (Acts 18:24–28; Rom. 16:3–4), but precisely Paul's endorsement of Stephanas suggests that many in the Corinthian congregation did not recognize him as such. It is probably best to envision a complex mixture of socioeconomic classes in the leadership of the house churches. At Corinth this produced a fragmented situation which, from Paul's point of view, climaxed in the congregation's misunderstanding of the Lord's Supper.

THE SUPPER OF DISCERNMENT

Paul writes to his Corinthian readers:

> When you come together, it is not the Lord's Supper that you eat. For in eating, each one goes ahead with his own meal, and one is hungry and another is drunk. What! Do you not have houses to eat and drink in? Or do you despise the church of God and humiliate those who have nothing? (1 Cor. 11:20–22)

Here Paul delivers himself of a severe judgment against his readers: They do not celebrate the true Supper of the Lord in their gatherings. What leads up to this apostolic pronouncement? In a nutshell, Paul believes that the sharing of food and drink at the congregational meal is not happening in such a way as to honor all members of the community. According to Paul, this defect alone causes the Corinthian celebration to become chiefly an occasion for judgment upon the participants (11:27–32). So real is the judgment that "many . . . are weak and ill, and some have died" (11:30). It is not that the supper itself has become meaningless. Paul agrees with his readers that the food and drink they consume are "spiritual" in the numinous sense (1 Cor. 10:1–4; 11:27). Where he differs from them, or at least from the offenders who proceed privately with their own meals, is in their conviction that these spiritual elements benefit them automatically, like a medicine. Therefore the apostle points out from Israel's history that those who eat and drink spiritually are obligated to behave in a God-pleasing manner and will be punished if they do not (10:5–11). At Corinth the chief sin, as Paul sees it, has to do with believers despising and humiliating one another in just that holy setting where they ought to be enhancing one another's worth.

Of course not all members of the church were equally at fault. The work of Gerd Theissen helps to show that this problem arose largely because some Corinthians failed to let the gospel touch their social and/or economic privileges. Piecing together items of information gleaned from the epistle as a whole, Theissen constructs a profile of the Corinthians who were most likely to have eaten their meals prematurely. If not many in the congregation were "wise according to wordly standards . . . powerful . . . [and] of noble birth" (1 Cor. 1:26), some nevertheless were. These, by and large, were the people wealthy enough to have "houses to eat and drink in." Moreover, this group would have taken the liberal position on eating meat offered to idols (1 Corinthians 8), for they were the only ones able to afford it on any regular basis. Theissen concludes: "It can be assumed that the conflict over the Lord's Supper is a conflict between rich and poor Christians."[17]

This summary of the matter should be accepted only with nuances. For example, Stephanas was probably a well-to-do householder, but Paul commends his behavior without reservation (16:15–18). In addition, it does not follow that the "wise according to worldly standards" were necessarily rich and therefore able to provide their own meals. Many slaves were highly educated but poor. Nevertheless, Theissen's insight provides a helpful cutting edge for our inquiry, and his reconstruction of events surrounding the congregational meal casts much light on the actual practice of hospitality in Corinth.

According to Theissen, the eucharistic sequence favored by Paul would have been roughly the following: (1) The gathering of the whole congregation—an extended process since some believers (e.g., slaves, apprentices, and dependent members of nonbelieving households) would have limited personal control over their time. (2) The preparation of food and drink for a common meal. Most of this would be donated by wealthier members of the congregation inasmuch as the poor had little or "nothing" to spare (11:22). (3) The utterance by a leader of Jesus' last supper words over the bread. This liturgical act would mark the beginning of a full meal utilizing the donated food. (4) The words over the wine, followed by the drinking of wine in common and some concluding blessings. The problem was that before the bread words were spoken certain wealthier Christians, with their households and supporters, had begun to consume portions of the food and wine they had brought with them for donation. This practice had the effect of diminishing the quantity of the fare to be served up for everyone at the Lord's table. In addition, it may well be that these offenders ate and drank the best of what they brought, thereby filling themselves to excess and lowering the quality of the holy meal for others. Thus "one [was] hungry and another . . . drunk" (11:21).[18]

But a further, more damaging consequence of the separate meals indulged in by the well-to-do and those who belonged to their circles was that other worshipers were being placed in an inferior social/ spiritual position—and this at what was supposed to be the Lord's own table. The separatists must have thought that because they themselves were furnishing most of the congregation's material resources, they had the right to skim off some cream from their milk before passing it around.[19] But this attitude made their table companions into recipients of their leftovers and second-class members of Christ's body. Having fought for equality at table in Antioch (Gal. 2:11–14), Paul now charges the separatists in Corinth with despising and humiliating their coworshipers.

The apostle does not ask his well-to-do readers to give up their economic advantage altogether. Instead, he tells them that if they want to feast in the manner of conventional society they should do so in their own houses (1 Cor. 11:22) on their own time. But the Lord's Supper must be a special demonstration of equality and reciprocity. Why? Clearly Paul thought of this supper as a generative symbol. Jesus himself had instituted the meal. Here the body which had given itself up on the cross, but now lived, and the church-body created by that death and resurrection were displaying their "communion" in a singular way (10:16). It was therefore here that the new humanity, freed by Christ from divisions of class, race, and sex, should be emerging most visibly from the present evil age. For Paul, the Lord's Supper had to be a real-life preview of the coming kingdom so that it could inspire other kinds of sharing in the church, both spiritual and material.

To make his point, Paul quotes what we have come to call the "words of institution" (11:23–26). These would have been well known to his readers in some form. But it looks as if the apostle has added two brief glosses to the common tradition so as to accent the tremendous price paid by Christ in giving birth to his church. The two expansions, most modern scholars believe, are the words "on the night when he was betrayed" (11:23b) and "For as often as you eat this bread and drink this cup, you proclaim the Lord's death until he comes" (11:26). Paul's interpolations have the effect of shaming those who treat the supper as a simple matter of filling themselves up with divine substance (see 11:27). For the apostle, an eating and drinking that proclaims the Lord's death is one that acts out the word of the cross socially. That is, the supper of the crucified Lord must disclose and embody God's world-reversing gospel. Here, as in Christ's death and resurrection, the weak, the lowly, the foolish, and the despised of the present age are being lifted up (1:26–29).

To facilitate the reception of this teaching, a hard one for all privileged people, Paul adds a further thought to his interpretation of the Lord's Supper. In his experience this common meal offers a unique opportunity for seeing oneself truly united with one's sisters and brothers in the mystery of Christ's body.

> Let a man [person] test himself out in practice *(dokimazein)* and so eat of the bread and drink of the cup. For anyone who eats and drinks without discerning *(diakrinein)* the body eats and drinks judgment *(krima)* upon himself. That is why many of you are weak and ill, and some have died. Now if we were in fact discerning *(diakrinein)* ourselves, we would not be currently under judgment *(krinein)*. But as it is, being judged *(krinein)* by the Lord, we are being disciplined so that we might not be condemned *(katakrinein)* with the world. (11:28–32; au. trans.)

Except for the first one, every Greek word transliterated above derives from a single verb, *krinein*. The prefix *dia-* changes its basic meaning from "judge" to "judge through and through" or "discern." The prefix *kata-* adds a pejorative dimension, hence "condemn." What is to be tested in practice and discerned is oneself-in-the body of Christ. Paul wants to help his readers toward a vision something like the following:

> I see now that I cannot be separate in the Lord from these, my brothers and sisters. They are sharers in Christ's body as real and valuable as I am. I am neither more nor less than they, but only different. I cannot use what the world counts as advantage against these people. We exist as partners and we need one another for the sake of our very lives.

Thus, a believer discerns the body primarily by acknowledging his or her unity with it, by honoring its wholeness in the person of each individual member,[20] and by expecting Christ, with his blessings and commands, to be present in all who partake of the holy meal. Paul has already introduced this truth in 1 Cor. 10:16–17: "The bread which we break, is it not a participation *(koinonia)* in the body of Christ? Because there is one bread, we who are many are one body." Then, in chapters 12–14, this partnership in Christ becomes the experiential core from which Paul derives his thoughts about the diversity and mutuality of spiritual gifts.

But if Christ is *not* welcomed by his people in one another, that is, if barriers are erected to obscure or prevent this hospitality, then he comes to the supper as a judging host whose food and drink have the effect of punishing his guests. However, even in this stern role, Paul hastens to add, Christ is more the savior than the magistrate. His underlying purpose is to purge, to shape what seems recalcitrant into the new humanity that it really is already by virtue of baptism (see 11:32, where the word translated "chastened" in the RSV is *paideuein,* the popular Greek term for "educate through discipline"). Thus Christ's judgment helps to save believers from condemnation "along with the world" by molding them back into his body even as they resist.

We should note here that Paul does not expect Christ's judgment, salutary as it is, to be the *normal* experience of those who gather for the Eucharist ("Now if we were in fact discerning ourselves, we would not be currently under judgment," 11:32; see also 11:34). "Discerning ourselves" is the normal experience, that is, the revelatory seeing of ourselves-in-the Body that prepares us for the Spirit's manifestations in our table companions. As modern interpreters, we perhaps need to remind ourselves that the whole purpose behind Paul's somber disser-tation on the Lord's Supper in 1 Corinthians is to open up for his readers a profound joy which they have been missing. The normal experience would be that of a lively giving and receiving among participants at the full meal which took place between the bread and cup words. One cannot help wondering whether the forms of the Holy Communion typically employed in our mainline churches can make space for this joyful mutuality, for this discernment of ourselves in the body and the communication (through prophecy?) of our renewed vision to our neighbors.

Near the end of his admonitions Paul writes, "So then, my brethren, when you come together to eat, wait for one another" (11:33). The last verb here is wonderfully ambiguous. On the most literal level it means "wait until everyone has come." But it can also mean (and surely does in this context) "wait with positive expecta-tions" (see 1 Cor. 16:11) or "receive" as one would a guest or visitor.[21] In other words, Paul urges his Corinthian readers to do essentially what he will later recommend to the believers at Rome: "Welcome one another." Within the new humanity Christ's supper of discern-ment provides an ongoing stimulus for the generation of new social relationships. In addition to these, however, and partly no doubt because of them, Paul discerns other patterns of exchange in Christ which are more properly termed economic. Three stories of material sharing associated with Paul's missionary enterprise serve to illustrate this dimension of New Testament hospitality.

THREE PARTNERSHIPS IN
THE GOSPEL

1. Paul himself knew the extremes of economic existence ("I have learned the secret of facing plenty and hunger, abundance and want," Phil. 4:12; see also 2 Cor. 6:5, 10). Although he was an educated man and a Roman citizen, he practiced, as an expression of his apostolic calling, the trade of the itinerant tentmaker. This marginal profession allowed him to mingle with classes of people, mostly lower, whom he might not have known otherwise.[22] Paul could not always earn enough to support himself, especially during periods of imprisonment, but it is noteworthy that only from a group of relatively poor Christians, the churches of Macedonia (2 Cor. 8:1–5), did he accept regular financial support. This came not as a monthly stipend but whenever Paul especially needed it and the Macedonians were able to raise it (Phil. 4:10, 14). Its regularity derived from the trust that he and his supporters had pledged to one another, a trust that took the form of a Roman trade institution called the *societas*. This was a contractual agreement by means of which members contributed their property, labor, skill, status, and so on, toward the achievement of a common goal.[23] Apparently Paul's *societas* with the Philippians came into being during his first visit when the central church of Macedonia was founded:

> And you Philippians yourselves know that in the beginning of the gospel, when I left Macedonia no church entered into partnership *(koinōnein)* with me in giving and receiving except you only, for even in Thessalonica you sent me help once and again. (Phil. 4:15–16)

The intriguing point here is that both sides believed this relationship to be a mutual one; for the Philippians as well as Paul it was a "giving and receiving."

What did the Philippians receive? One obvious answer would be their new life in Christ and the nurturing of it under Paul's leadership. But the apostle's letter to Philippi shows that this was not all. The Philippians have a "partnership in the gospel" (1:5), which means that they join in the triumphant work of God to redeem the entire world (see, e.g., 2:5–11; 3:10–17). Their voluntary agreement to support the apostle grants them a special status in this work: to be with him in his words and acts and sufferings, wherever these occur, "to advance the gospel" (4:12–14; 1:12). The Philippians are doing God's work through Paul, and God does not forget their effort. The apostle assures them, "Not that I seek the gift [money or provisions from Philippi recently sent to him in prison at Ephesus[24]]; but I seek the fruit which increases to your credit. . . . And my God will supply every need of yours according to his riches in glory in Christ Jesus" (4:17, 19). Here we find a three-way reciprocity. The contractual relationship between Paul and the Philippians is really a compact made by both parties with God. Paul writes playfully, for he does not wish to push the image of God as accountant too far (see Rom. 4:1–11). Nevertheless, he uses business language, well understood by the Philippians, to bring home the point that God is pleased with their efforts and will always provide them with sufficient resources from the heavenly wealth which they are already beginning to experience "in Christ Jesus." The Philippians have sent their gift to Paul, but by virtue of their special partnership in the gospel, they have really sent it to God. It is a "fragrant offering, a sacrifice acceptable" (4:18).

We do not know exactly how Paul and the Philippians entered into this special partnership. The apostle does not believe it to be normative for all congregations founded by him (4:15–16; 1 Cor. 9:12–18). It must have appeared to both parties as a charismatic gift/task granted specifically to them (see Rom. 12:8, where Paul identifies liberal giving as a *charisma*). Perhaps the merchants of the congregation, people like Lydia (Acts 16:11–15), proposed it to their apostle after thinking through how the gospel had begun to reshape their everyday vocations. In any case we do have a cameo description by Paul of the way his Macedonian friends embarked upon another sharing project, namely, the collection he and his Gentile congregations were gathering for poor believers in the church at Jerusalem. And this time, writing to the Corinthians, Paul does hold up the behavior of his most faithful supporters as an example:

> We want you to know, brothers and sisters, about the grace *(charin)* of God given to the churches of Macedonia, for in a great testing of affliction the abundance of their joy and their deep poverty combined to multiply into a wealth of generosity on their part, so that according to their means, I testify, and beyond their means, of their own free will,

with much beseeching they kept asking us for the favor of partnership in the ministry to the saints *(tēn charin kai tēn koinōnian tēs diakonias tēs eis tous hagious);* and not as we expected, but first they gave themselves to the Lord and then to us. (2 Cor. 8:1–5; au. trans.)

Some of the thoughts presented here bear a striking resemblance to those occurring in Phil. 4:14–20. In the matter of this special collection for Jerusalem, as in their relationship with Paul generally, the Macedonian Christians wish to form a partnership. Moreover, they do so as an act (or consequence) of worship. The new thought here is that this process begins with a self-offering, first to Christ and then, according to the terms of their *societas* with Paul, to him as well. Only then do the Macedonians begin to count out the actual monetary amount of their contribution and get down to logistical details. With such faith and loyalty and generosity these believers constructed an effective home base for their traveling apostle, even when he was far away from them. In fact, they became agents of God's hospitality to him, and through him to the world.

Something akin to Paul's partnership with the Macedonians on behalf of the poor was reported in a recent issue of a denominational journal. The event took place a few years ago when Dr. Carl Mau of the Lutheran World Federation received permission to visit a congregation of "Volga Germans," deported from Moscow in the 1930s to their present home in Karaganda, Siberia. Until 1976 they had had no personal contact with people from outside the U.S.S.R. During a sermon by Dr. Mau, which included the detail that nearly one-half of the world's population suffers from hunger, people began to break down and cry. They had never heard about this tragic situation. Immediately after the service elders of the congregation held a meeting and decided on the spot to donate half the church's treasury, about sixteen thousand dollars, to help alleviate world hunger. They were saddened to learn of the law that prohibits Soviet currency from being taken out of the country for such purposes.[25]

2. The collection for Jerusalem referred to above was itself a twin act of worship and hospitality. Paul describes it to the Romans as follows:

For Macedonia and Achaia were pleased to take up a certain partner's contribution *(koinōnia)* for the poor among the saints in Jerusalem.

> They were pleased and are in fact in debt to them. For if the Gentiles
> have become partakers with them *(koinōnein)* of their spiritual goods
> *(pneumatika)*, they ought also to perform a service for them with mate-
> rial goods. (Rom. 15:26–27; au. trans.)

The idea behind this description is that Gentile believers, by offering
themselves to God (15:16) and their material gifts to their Jewish
Christian brothers and sisters, are enacting a type or preview of the
end-time events foretold in Isa. 60:1–7; 66:20. There the prophet sees
Israel, blessed with a visitation of God's glory in Jerusalem, drawing
to itself all nations, with their material resources. Early Christian
experience had to modify this picture in that it saw God's glory in
Christ already moving out from Jerusalem to meet the nations on
their own ground. Thus Paul conceives of his collection, begun at the
request of the Jerusalem church (Gal. 2:10), as a response to grace, a
repayment for goods already received.

But much more than this is at stake. Paul believes that when the
guests of God from Gentile nations come bearing gifts to the people
of God in Jerusalem, the resulting exchange will enable both parties
to worship together and welcome one another (at table?) in ways that
so far they have been unable to do:

> For the rendering of this service not only supplies the wants of the saints
> but also overflows in many thanksgivings to God. Under the test of this
> service you [Corinthians] will glorify God by your obedience in acknowl-
> edging the gospel of Christ and by the generosity of your contribution
> . . . while they [the Jerusalem Christians] long for you and pray for you
> because of the surpassing grace of God in you. (2 Cor. 9:12–14)

What Paul foresees here is a new stage of partnership with strangers.
He knows firsthand about the mistrust that still divides Jewish believers from their Gentile brothers and sisters. Given the symbolic
value attached by the apostle to this collection and his careful assembling of it over the period of some years (for it was no emergency
measure), we must presume that he expected it somehow to hasten
the ingathering of "the full number of the Gentiles," the completion
of which would mark Christ's visible return to earth (Rom. 11:25–26;
15:28–29).[26]

Although believers at Corinth eventually took part in the collection
(Rom. 15:26), they proved to be quite slow about readying their
contribution for delivery to Jerusalem (2 Corinthians 8—9).[27] Among

the reasons for their footdragging was a belief, common enough among people who have achieved a moderate degree of material security, that their own needs demanded most of their resources. The apostle addresses this fear of scarcity first of all by humbling his readers with the example of the poor but generous Macedonians (8:1–5; see also 9:2–5). But then follows a second argument in chapters 8–9 directed to the fear of the Corinthians that they do not have enough to share. It proceeds from Paul's conviction that all Christians are presently rich through God's grace and destined to receive even more divine wealth in the future. Thus he reminds his readers that they "excel in everything—in faith, in utterance, in knowledge, in all earnestness, and in your love for us" (8:7). This is the abundance won for the Corinthians by Christ, who "though he was rich, yet for your sake . . . became poor, so that by his poverty you might become rich" (8:9). With his talent for paradox Paul makes this motto work on at least three levels. The richness earned by Christ for the Corinthians is not just future; they have some of it even now. But because it is *Christ's* richness they enjoy, they must offer it up, as he did, to make others wealthy (2 Cor. 6:10). And yet it never really disappears because God's abundance prevails over all scarcity, as the raising of Christ from poverty to lordship makes clear. God's wealth multiplies for those who put their partnership with the crucified and risen Christ to material use. Here we come to the core of Paul's argument throughout 2 Corinthians 8—9. "The point is this: he who sows sparingly will also reap sparingly, and he who sows bountifully will also reap bountifully" (9:6, a paraphrase of Prov. 11:24).

The apostle is quite straightforward about the self-interest inherent in this argument. He does not expect the Corinthians to impoverish themselves from their giving (8:13). On the contrary, he expects them to gain from it, indeed, gain from it in the giving itself, which is to be done freely, cheerfully, and in a variety of ways to be determined by individuals on the basis of their resources (8:12; 9:7). As always, the foundation for this plenitude is the ever-present divine wealth, for

> God is able to provide you with every blessing in abundance, so that you may always have enough of everything and may provide in abundance for every good work. . . . He who supplied seed to the sower and bread for food will supply and multiply your resources and increase the harvest of

your righteousness. You will be enriched in every way for great generosity. (9:8, 10–11)

In Iris Murdoch's novel *The Bell* the Abbess of Imber puts this presumption of faith into more contemporary clothing.

Remember that [God] will in his own way and in his own time complete what we so poorly attempt. Often we do not achieve for others the good that we intend; but we achieve something, something that goes on from our effort. Good is an overflow. Where we generously and sincerely intend it, we are engaged in a work of creation.[28]

To take up their roles in this work of the Lord, the Corinthians are asked by Paul to enter into a new relationship, both with the Jerusalem Christians and with God. Here Paul's exchanges with the Philippians come into play once again, for it is no coincidence that he calls the collection for Jerusalem a *koinōnia* (2 Cor. 8:4; 9:13) and a *charis* (8:4, 6, 7, 19). Except for 8:4, this second word is translated "gracious work" in the RSV, but such a rendering obscures the fact that elsewhere in chapters 8–9 *charis* always refers to *God's* acts and blessings, that is, God's investment in the partnership (see 8:19; 9:8, 14) or profit from it, as in the expression "thanks be to God" (8:16; 9:15).

One special gain from this partnership for the human participants will be a new kind of equity:

For it is not that others should enjoy ease while you suffer tribulations, but that from equality *(ex isotētos)* in the present time your abundance might flow toward what they lack so that their abundance might emerge for what you lack, in order that equality might occur. (8:13–14; au. trans.)

In this rather obscure passage it is nevertheless clear that Paul advises a redistribution of material goods. The Corinthians, who are relatively well off as a congregation, should donate some of their money and provisions to help the poverty-stricken Jerusalem church. The apostle does not ask his readers to calculate their gift so that they and the believers in Palestine will henceforth live on exactly the same economic level. The word "equality" means something else, namely, that in God's plan the sum total of spiritual and material gifts on each side should be the same. This can never be tabulated by means of conventional arithmetic, but it will be achieved by God's redistribution through sharing among Christians.[29] The point is not that believers in Jerusalem will return the Corinthians' material favor at some future time. Rather, Paul sees the *current exchange* as a giving of both sides from their abundance and a receiving of both sides from their respective poverties.

The Corinthians are to initiate this sharing, but Paul predicts that even as their gift is delivered they will experience a deeper level of acceptance from the mother church. They will witness a glorification of God for their work by the Jerusalem believers; and this in turn will open, perhaps once and for all, the gates that have prevented Jews and Gentiles in the church from sitting down together as a community of equals:

> Through the proof which this ministry furnishes they will glorify God for the obedience of your confession to Christ's gospel and for the generosity of your ministry toward them and toward all. And they will long for you with prayer on your behalf because of the overwhelming grace of God active in you. (9:13–14; au. trans.)

Thus the Corinthians' immediate gain from their sharing will be a sociospiritual welcome from the Jerusalem church which advances the gospel. Although she is not commenting specifically on 2 Corinthians 8—9, Letty Russell catches the spirit of Paul's argument when she notes that partnerships in the New Creation always "draw us together in *common struggle* and work, involving risk, continuing growth, and hopefulness in moving toward a goal or purpose transcending the group. By definition, partnership involves growing interdependence."[30]

But there is still another way to understand the profit that will result from the partnership urged by Paul, and that is from God's point of view. God "spends" grace to equip Christians for sharing (2 Cor. 8:1, 9; 9:8, 14). Then, as they take up their task and put grace to work in an exchange of gifts, the human members of the partnership generate an overflow toward God:

> You will be enriched . . . for great generosity, which through us will produce thanksgiving to God; for the rendering of this service not only supplies the wants of the saints but overflows in many thanksgivings to God. . . . [the Jerusalem believers] will glorify God by your obedience. . . . Thanks *(charis)* be to God for his inexpressible gift. (2 Cor. 9:11–13, 15)

God, the multiplier of gifts, invests grace *(charis)* in the enterprise of the gospel and receives it back again in the form of ever-growing thanksgivings (see 2 Cor. 4:15). Or, to translate this circular flow more directly into the language of our study: the worldwide hospitality of believers, one to another, expands their ability to welcome God with their praises. The new humanity matures, and God reaps benefits.

3. Paul's short personal letter to the Christian slaveowner Philemon provides yet another variation on the theme of hospitable sharing in Christ, this time with an unmistakably comic element. The story is well known but bears repetition. Paul, writing from prison (probably in Ephesus), has granted refuge to Philemon's runaway slave Onesimus. The latter comes, or comes back to faith in Christ under the apostle's pastoral care. Paul then writes Philemon, whom he has previously known as a friend and fellow worker, urging that he welcome Onesimus to his household "no longer as a slave, but as a beloved brother" (v. 16). There are strong hints that Paul is also asking for Onesimus to be sent to him as a helper once the hoped-for reconciliation with Philemon takes place (13–14, 20–21). The picture presented in Col. 4:7–9, where a person named Onesimus appears to be a traveling missionary, suggests that Philemon complied with Paul's requests.[31]

The language of hospitality abounds in this letter, much of it taking the form of wordplays directed to Philemon's sense of humor—and this in a situation where he probably thinks of himself as the wronged party (see v.18). Paul begins by offering profuse compliments to his "beloved fellow worker" (v. 1). Not only does Philemon make his home available to a house church (v. 2); he has also proved himself to be a specialist in hospitality who shows love and faithfulness toward "all the saints," refreshing their hearts *(splanchna)* as well as their bodies (vv. 4, 6). This probably means that Philemon has earned a reputation for providing welcomes to Christian travelers characterized by the sharing of spiritual gifts (as in Rom. 1:11–12).

Paul builds his appeal for Onesimus on precisely this reputation. The apostle would have preferred to keep Onesimus with him "in order that he might serve me on your behalf during my imprisonment for the gospel" (v. 13). Nevertheless, in compliance with the law of the empire and the principle of respect for his fellow worker Philemon, he is sending the runaway back. He makes appeals on

Onesimus's behalf, but for the sake of friendship he eschews any fuller use of his apostolic authority (8–14). Careful modern readers will be quick to perceive the manipulative effect of this excessive politeness. And so, almost certainly, did Philemon! Toward the end of his short letter the apostle finally drops all pretense:

> (15) Perhaps this is why he was parted from you for a while, that you might have him back forever, (16) no longer as a slave but more than a slave, as a beloved brother, especially to me but how much more to you, both in the flesh and in the Lord. (17) So if you consider me your partner *(koinōnos)*, receive him as you would receive me. (18) If he has wronged you at all, or owes you anything, charge that to my account. (19) I, Paul, write this with my own hand, I will repay it—to say nothing of your owing me even your own self. (20) Yes, brother, I want some benefit *(onaimēn*: a word play on the name Onesimus, which itself means "useful") from you in the Lord. Refresh my heart *(splanchna)* in Christ. (21) Confident of your obedience, I write to you, knowing that you will do even more than I say.

Here the screw turns, but not without laughter. Philemon, the expert in hospitality, is bidden to receive his own slave as a guest, indeed as an emissary from the apostle who must be honored as the latter's own presence. Paul's signed pledge that he will redress all financial grievances from his own pocket must have sounded ludicrous coming from a migrant tentmaker in prison. On the other hand, to balance *everything* up, including spiritual debts, there was that little matter of Philemon's owing Paul "his own self" (perhaps a reference to Philemon's conversion). In v. 20 the apostle states his purpose openly: from the talented host Philemon he wants some refreshment for his own heart. But this now means Onesimus as well as Paul, for in v. 12 the runaway has been referred to as "my very *splanchna*."

In v. 17 hospitality language merges with the business language of partnership. It seems that Paul has made some previous sharing arrangement with Philemon, not unlike his *societas* with the Philippians. Thus he can refer to Philemon's practice of hospitality as a *koinōnia* which includes Christ and the apostle as well as the travelers being refreshed (vv. 5–7). On this basis Paul can exhort Philemon to perform his share of "*all* the good that is ours in Christ" (v. 6; emphasis added). Moreover, the apostle can presume upon his own status as a partner when he asks that the whole matter of Onesimus be charged to his account (v. 18). Just as he had done with the

Corinthians, Paul here argues that his solution will produce gain for all parties, especially for Philemon himself (vv. 15–16). In a final bit of bravado the apostle suggests that this gain will be multiplied not many days hence when he comes to pay Philemon a visit: "By the way, get a guest room ready for me; for I am expecting that through the prayers of you and yours God will grant me to you" (v. 22; au. trans.).

Does the apostle expect his fellow worker to free Onesimus? The answer is not entirely clear; but when Philemon is advised to welcome the fugitive back "no longer as a slave but more than a slave, as a beloved brother . . . both in the flesh and in the Lord" (v. 16), the last phrase especially seems to envision a transformed relationship between the two men which is to take place not only before God in worship but also in the everyday socioeconomic world. When we add to this strong hint Paul's confidence that Philemon will "do even more than I say" (v. 21), it becomes quite likely that the apostle has a total manumission from slavery in mind.

In any case, the letter to Philemon shows us once again that for Paul every act of hospitality by believers takes place on both the spiritual and physical levels. Each event, when followed to its conclusion, produces socioeconomic results. At the same time, in and with every transaction the mysterious presence of Christ leads guests and hosts alike toward "all the good" that they are meant to share as his partners (v. 6; note the recurrence of "in Christ" or "in the Lord" throughout Philemon, e.g., vv. 6, 8, 16, 20, 23). It seems altogether fitting for Paul to close his letter by wishing his partner-host the ultimate refreshment: "The grace of the Lord Jesus Christ be with your spirit" (v. 25).

By way of summary, we may say that the three partnerships described above show themselves to be economic in nature because they all involve some transaction within the material order. At the same time, however, these givings and receivings are spiritual insofar as God or Christ acts through them to multiply benefits for all sides. Such benefits cannot always be defined in advance with great clarity, but in Paul's view they are never less real than matter itself. Paul would probably subscribe to the view that "the best things in life aren't things." By the same token, he would also insist that Christ's redemption of the material world must produce socioeconomic changes in the relationships of believers.

Finally, we should note that it is a matter of definition whether or not the three alliances just described should be thought of in terms of partnership with strangers. Paul knows the Philippians well and feels great affection for them. The churches of Macedonia and Achaia, who join with their apostle in assembling the collection for Jerusalem, may be understood as friendly competitors. Likewise, Philemon and Paul seem to have cooperated for years before the apostle wrote his letter. Should we speak of strangers when the parties concerned are so well known to each other? On the other hand, each of the Pauline partnerships examined includes God and Christ, which automatically means that unexpected results will occur, for example, that the human partners must be ready to receive one another in novel ways and take on new roles themselves. In effect, the letters to Philippi, Corinth, and Philemon "up the ante" in relationships between Paul and the respective readers. Moreover, each of these partnerships is designed to reach out to include others. From the Philippians, Paul wants to gain further support for the "progress of the gospel" among Gentiles. With the Corinthians his objective is to bring about their wholehearted participation in the collecton so that Jewish and Gentile believers can accept one another more fully and experience new vigor in their combined mission to the world. By analogy, the partnership into which Philemon and Paul have entered must now incorporate the marginal figure Onesimus so that he can become a co-worker in ministry, most likely as Paul's companion. On balance, it is fair to conclude that the apostle's thinking about socioeconomic exchanges among believers is pervaded by a sensitivity toward strangers.

If we review the earlier sections of this chapter, we find that much the same interpretation may be placed upon Paul's strenuous efforts to produce inclusive table fellowship in Antioch, Rome, and Corinth. For him, the gospel itself suffers violence in situations that do not permit an openness to deeper forms of sharing. Only as believers acknowledge the strangers in their midst and reach out to welcome one another can grace abound for the world. According to the apostle, this is the new humanity in action, the house of God a-building.

All of Paul's teachings about the church, the kingdom, the body of Christ, and even justification by grace cluster about this image of welcoming and fan out from it. If Paul's vision corresponds to reality, the home we all long for is as close to us as a guest-host relationship with our neighbor in Christ.

NOTES

1. While it is true that Luke has shaped the two narratives editorially, one can argue that he did not simply create them from his own theological reflections but rather built upon traditional reports, perhaps by eyewitnesses. According to Robert Jewett, this form of composition is most evident in Acts when Luke gives detailed information about Paul's journeys and/or periods of residence, as in our two stories. See *A Chronology of Paul's Life* (Philadelphia: Fortress Press, 1979), 7–22, 51, 102. Fitzmyer, in *The Gospel According to Luke I–IX*, presents plausible evidence for regarding Luke as a sometime collaborator of Paul who would have known him personally. See 47–51.

2. Robert Jewett, *Christian Tolerance: Paul's Message to the Modern Church* (Philadelphia: Westminster Press, 1982), 24–36.

3. I take Romans 16 as an integral part of the apostle's original letter to believers in the imperial capital. See Harry Y. Gamble, Jr., *The Textual History of the Letter to the Romans* (Grand Rapids: Wm. B. Eerdmans, 1971); Karl Paul Donfried, "A Short Note on Romans 16," in *The Romans Debate*, ed. K. P. Donfried (Minneapolis: Augsburg Pub. House, 1977), 50–60; Raymond E. Brown and John P. Meier, *Rome and Antioch: New Testament Cradles of Catholic Christianity* (New York: Paulist Press, 1983), 106–9.

4. Jewett, *Christian Tolerance*, 29.

5. For a more extensive treatment of spiritual gifts, especially in the Pauline congregations, see my *Charismata: God's Gifts for God's People* (Philadelphia: Westminster Press, 1978).

6. Robert Banks, *Paul's Idea of Community: The Early House Churches in Their Historical Setting* (Grand Rapids: Wm. B. Eerdmans, 1980), 141.

7. Wayne A. Meeks, *The First Urban Christians: The Social World of the Apostle Paul* (New Haven, Conn.: Yale Univ. Press, 1983), 191.

8. Ibid., 191.

9. Ibid., 192.

10. Alan Paton, *Ah, But Your Land Is Beautiful* (New York: Charles Scribner's Sons, 1981), 235.

11. P. Stuhlmacher, "Urchristliche Hausgemeinden," in *Der Brief an Philemon*, EKK (Zürich: Benziger Verlag, 1975), 72. The number ten derives from the *minyan* or quorum of men required for the formation of a synagogue. The larger number results from archaeological investigations into

the typical maximum size of Greco-Roman houses during the first-century period. On the latter, see also Banks, *Paul's Idea of Community*, 41–42.

12. Stuhlmacher, "Urchristliche Hausgemeinden," 72–75.

13. Malherbe, "House Churches and Their Problems," in *Social Aspects of Early Christianity*, 88–91; and Sampley, *Pauline Partnership in Christ*, esp. 51–115.

14. See, e.g., Henry Bettenson, ed., *Documents of the Christian Church* (New York: Oxford Univ. Press, 1960 [1947]), 5–7; and Daniel J. Theron, *Evidence of Tradition* (Grand Rapids: Baker Book House, 1958), 12–17.

15. Banks, *Paul's Idea of Community*, 80–89.

16. See n. 11 above. The Pentecost story narrated in Acts 2 seems to contain evidence for a considerably larger dwelling. Luke reports that about 120 people (1:15) "were all together in one place," namely, "the house where they were sitting" (2:1–2). But as the story unfolds it becomes evident that Luke has in mind some kind of building with an open courtyard. The local populace does not have to enter the house to find out what is going on. Nor does Peter "come out" to speak to the crowd.

17. Gerd Theissen, *The Social Setting of Pauline Christianity: Essays on Corinth*, trans. J. H. Schütz (Philadelphia: Fortress Press, 1982), 151. See the entire essay, "Social Integration and Sacramental Activity: An Analysis of 1 Cor. 11:17–34," 145–74.

18. Ibid., 151–163.

19. Ibid., 153–156. See esp. p. 171 n. 20.

20. This is nicely explicated by Northrup Frye in *The Great Code: The Bible and Literature* (New York: Harcourt Brace Jovanovich, 1981), 166–68.

21. W. Grundmann, *"Dechomai,"* et. al., *TDNT*, 2:56; and Banks, *Paul's Idea of Community*, 63.

22. Ronald F. Hock, *The Social Context of Paul's Ministry: Tentmaking and Apostleship* (Philadelphia: Fortress Press, 1980), 66–68.

23. Sampley, *Pauline Partnership in Christ*, 11–20; 51–77. See also my *Philippians and Philemon*, ACNT (Minneapolis: Augsburg Pub. House, 1985).

24. For a discussion of the location from which Paul wrote Philippians, see the introduction to this epistle in my *Philippians and Philemon*.

25. Edgar R. Trexler, "Editor's Opinion," *The Lutheran* 19 (1981), 34.

26. Keith F. Nickle thinks that Paul intended the collection to effect a massive conversion of Jews to faith in Christ. See *The Collection: A Study in Paul's Strategy* (London: SCM Press, 1966), 155–56. This seems unlikely in light of Rom. 15:25–32 where the apostle, anticipating his trip to Jerusalem to hand over the collection, hopes only for deliverance from Jewish "unbelievers." On the other hand, he very much wants and expects Jewish believers in Jerusalem to find the gift he bears "acceptable." This positive reception would apply, of course, not only to the collection itself but also to Paul's whole missionary enterprise and its fruits, the Gentile believers of the

congregations he has founded (see 15:15–20). If Jewish Christians in Jerusalem do welcome these believers on a deeper level (especially those accompanying Paul), the apostle can look forward to strengthened support of the Gentile mission everywhere and hence to an increasing rate of Gentile conversions. Dieter Georgi comes close to this interpretation but does not spell it out in terms of an expectation on Paul's part that Christ's coming will be hastened by a successful outcome in Jerusalem. See *Die Geschichte der Kollekte des Paulus für Jerusalem* (Hamburg: Herbert Reich-Evangelischer Verlag, 1965), 65, 86–87.

27. For a convincing argument in favor of locating these two chapters in a single letter, written prior to chap. 10–13, see C. K. Barrett, *The Second Epistle to the Corinthians* (New York: Harper & Row, 1973), 11–21.

28. Iris Murdoch, *The Bell* (London: Triad/Granada, 1981), 235.

29. On the basis of parallel material from Philo, Georgi understands the phrase *ex isotētos* as virtually equivalent to "from God" or "from God's grace." See *Die Geschichte*, 64–65. According to Luke T. Johnson, this equality "is not the erasing of differences but the alternation of attentive care." See *Sharing Possessions: Symbol and Mandate of Faith* (Philadelphia: Fortress Press, 1981), 113.

30. Letty Russell, *Growth in Partnership* (Philadelphia: Westminster Press, 1981), 29.

31. For more details on this scenario, see my *Philippians and Philemon*.

CHAPTER 4

Guests and Hosts, Together in Mission (Luke)

Contemporary research into the two-volume work we call Luke-Acts has shown that this impressive piece of literature, which accounts for more than one-quarter of the New Testament, comes to us from an author with multiple intentions. Above all, Luke was concerned to encourage his readers with the "fuller knowledge" (*epiginōskein;* Luke 1:4; 24:16, 31) that their faith rested securely upon God's ancient relationship with Israel, a relationship that was now moving toward its providential fulfillment in history through Jesus and the Spirit (Acts 1:1–11). Within the framework of this broad purpose Luke also wanted to equip his readers for more effective participation in God's mission to the Greco-Roman world, while at the same time preparing them to withstand the persecutions that would result from their vigorous proclamation of the gospel. Jesus and Paul were to be their primary models for both endeavors.[1]

Woven together with Luke's primary intentions are a number of subthemes which may be regarded as distinctive to the Third Gospel and Acts. Among these we find emphases upon the harmonious interaction of believers, the singular contributions of women disciples, the continuing validity of God's covenant with the Jewish people,[2] the centrality of repentance in the life of faith, the just use of material possessions, and, especially in the Gospel segment of Luke-Acts, God's compassionate care for the poor and outcast. It may be argued that Luke's interest in hospitality is best understood as another of these subthemes.[3]

On the other hand, the sheer quantity of evidence for our author's regular accentuation of guest and host roles in his two-volume work suggests that the whole matter is more than peripheral to his concerns. Indeed, Paul Minear has proposed that for Luke "table fellowship as interpreted by table talk *constituted the gospel*" (emphasis added).[4] Is Minear's summary an exaggeration? A preliminary review of data relating to the interaction between guests and hosts in Luke-Acts will help us move toward formulating a satisfactory answer to this question. As our study proceeds, we shall find that Luke highlights hospitality in order to help residential believers, whose faith and life are centered in house church communities, take their rightful place alongside itinerant prophets in the worldwide mission initiated by Jesus. Luke wants to facilitate mutual welcoming between wanderers and residents so that all can share in the prophetic vocation. For him, cooperation is the key to missionary success. To achieve it, frequent reversals of guest and host roles among believers prove necessary; and these in turn often require repentance. Residential communities, particularly meal settings, are thought by Luke to be the primary locus for such interactions. To explore this hypothesis, we begin with a summary of the material in Luke-Acts that pertains to the theme of hospitality.

LUKE'S FOCUS ON HOSPITALITY

The very structure of Luke's work witnesses to a conviction on his part that some deep link exists between the verbal content of God's good news and its historical embodiment in boundary situations involving guests and hosts. Thus, our author narrates the birth of Jesus as follows:

> And while they were [in Bethlehem] the time came for her to be delivered. And she gave birth to her first-born son and wrapped him in swaddling clothes, and laid him in a manger, because there was no room for them in the inn. (Luke 2:6–7)

The king messiah is born in the city of David according to prophecy; but this happens in a way that marks him from the very beginning as a marginal person in Israel who has no proper dwelling place. It becomes clear, as Luke's Gospel story unfolds, that Jesus' true home is a heavenly one (Luke 9:16; 23:42–43; Acts 2:29–36). Although he assumes a real human body, his life on earth is that of a stranger. In contrast to Mark and Matthew, Luke allows Jesus no regular headquarters in Peter's house at Capernaum. Moreover, from 9:51 to 19:28, in the so-called "travel narrative" unique to the Third Gospel, he portrays him as one constantly on the road, sometimes finding hospitality with others (10:38–42; 11:37–54; 14:1–24; 19:1–10), sometimes experiencing rejection (9:52–53; 13:31, 34–35).

In a similar manner the Acts of the Apostles may be read, structurally, as a collection of guest and host stories about the missionary ventures generated in the Spirit-led communities of Jerusalem and Antioch. Often the names of individuals are reported for no other reason, it seems, than to point up their exemplary hospitality to such notable figures as Peter, Paul, Barnabas, and so on. This holds true, for example, with Judas (9:11), Simon the tanner (9:43; 10:6), Mary the mother of Mark (12:12), Jason (17:5–9), Titius Justus (18:7), Mnason (21:16), Julius (27:1–3), and the inhabitants of Malta, especially their "chief man" Publius (28:1–10). Other hosts play the additional roles of prominent converts or evangelists in their own right. In the first category we may place Cornelius (chaps. 10–11), Sergius Paulus (13:7–12), Lydia (16:14–15, 40), and the jailer of Philippi, with his family (16:25–34). To the second group belong Priscilla and Aquila (18:1–4) and Philip (21:8–14).

Consistent with Luke's stress in Acts upon cooperation between guests and hosts is the attention he gives to two remarkable pioneers of the early church: Joseph, "surnamed by the apostles Barnabas" (4:36), and Ananias of Damascus, the intermediary chosen by God for Saul's reception into the church (9:10–19). Both men are pictured as adventurers of faith who take risks to establish connections between Saul and their brother-sister believers, most of whom fear this notorious persecutor of the church or doubt the authenticity of his conversion (9:10–28). In other words, both of these individuals perform a ministry of hospitality which we might call bridge building.[5] The believers at Ephesus also exercise a version of this ministry when they write a letter of introduction on behalf of the Alexandrian disciple Apollos to the church at Corinth (18:24–28). For Luke, partnership with strangers becomes a natural feature of mission.

Finally, in terms of structure, the concluding verses of Acts seem carefully fashioned to balance the paradoxical birth of Jesus. For the Messiah, there was no room in the inn. For Paul, there was no access to the synagogues or churches of Rome. Instead, the apostle has to live under house arrest in quarters rented with his own funds. In this circumstance too, however, the saving plan of God finds special opportunity:

> And [Paul] lived there two whole years at his own expense and welcomed [i.e., received as guests] all who came to him, preaching the kingdom of God and teaching about the Lord Jesus Christ quite openly and unhindered. (28:30–31; see our previous comment on these verses above)

The word of the Lord grows (6:7; 12:24; 19:20), that is, moves progressively through the plane of human history. If its proclaimers are not entirely at home in that history, they nevertheless sanctify it by inviting their neighbors to savor the kingdom's advent. In doing so, they are extending *God's* invitation, for in Luke's view it is the Holy One of Israel who opens the "door of faith" to outsiders (14:27).

When we turn to the place of meals in Luke-Acts, we find that our author has assigned them an extraordinary prominence. For example, only in the Third Gospel does Jesus engage in table talk with Pharisees (7:36–50; 11:37–54; 14:1–24). Moreover, Luke's version of the last supper has been greatly expanded to include instructions spoken by Jesus at table to his disciples. Some of these have been taken over from Mark, who transmits them in other settings, but many are distinctive to Luke. Also unique to our Third Gospel are: the incident at Martha's house in which Mary is praised for her attentiveness to Jesus' table talk (10:38–42); the conversion of the chief tax collector Zaccheus, to whose house Jesus invites himself for the day (19:1–10); the story of the risen Christ's self-disclosure to two Emmaus-bound disciples "in the breaking of bread" (24:28–35); and the account of his appearance later that same day to a larger group of followers in which he establishes his identity by eating a piece of broiled fish before them (24:36–49). Finally, we should remember that in Luke's version of the Lord's Prayer the petition for bread is directly linked with the coming of the kingdom, probably in communal meal settings (see 11:2–4 and chap. 2 above).

Intertwined with these narratives are a large number of Lukan sayings by Jesus *about* table sharing (or the life and work of disciples for which table sharing stands as a symbol). Thus, only in the Third Gospel do we find parables depicting the rich fool, who wants no more than to "eat, drink and be merry" (12:16–21), the prodigal son, who experiences the fullness of his repentance at a magnificent banquet (15:11–32), and the wealthy householder, who denies poor Lazarus even the scraps from his table (16:19–31). Other sayings that relate to meals and that Luke alone transmits occur in 7:44–46; 11:5–8; 12:35–37, 41–48 (a variation on Q); 13:24–28; 14:7–14; 17:7–10; 22:27, 28–30 (a variation on Q).

For its part, Acts also contains an impressive number of references to meals. These are preceded by the almost casual observation that Jesus' followers dined with him on several occasions during the forty days between his resurrection and ascension (the best text of Acts 1:4 reads: "And while eating with them . . . "; see also 10:41). Henceforth, *koinōnia* at table becomes the socioreligious hallmark of the young Jerusalem church (2:42, 46). With good reason one modern interpreter names this first group of residential believers "the Lukan banquet community."[6] Here it is clear that Luke sees repentance and conversion as the acceptance of an invitation to take part in Christ's joyful feast of the end time (2:37–47). For him, the table and the kingdom of the Lord Jesus are virtually synonymous (Luke 22:30 and 14:15–24, where the last verse refers to Jesus' banquet, offered in the church's mission). For other meals in Acts where the believing community is understood to be mediating the lordship of Christ, see 6:1–3; 9:18–27; 10:1—11:3; 16:25–43; 20:7–10; 27:33–36; 28:30–31.

These stories from Luke-Acts may have been on Frederick Buechner's mind as he was spinning out the prototypical meal scene in his novel *Love Feast*. In this vignette, which very much resembles the great banquet of Luke 14:15–24, protagonist Leo Bebb, traveling evangelist and confidence man, hosts a Thanksgiving dinner at the Princeton, New Jersey home of his wealthy friend and patroness Gertrude Conover. The meal is a spur-of-the-moment affair whose guests are a strange combination of local residents, nuns, secretaries (at least one of whom is a part-time hooker), and students not otherwise occupied for the holiday. Some have been "compelled" to come in through aggressive invitations. When most of the guests have eaten their fill and consumed generous portions of Gertrude Conover's claret punch, Bebb addresses them. Antonio Parr, the novel's narrator, recalls the following fragments of Bebb's talk:

He said, "The Kingdom of Heaven is like a great feast. That's the way of it. The Kingdom of Heaven is a love feast where nobody's a stranger. Like right here. There's strangers everywhere you can think of. There's strangers was born out of the same womb. There's strangers was raised together in the same town and worked side by side all their life through. There's strangers got married and been climbing in and out of the same fourposter together for thirty-five or forty years, and they're strangers still. And Jesus, it's like most of the time he's a stranger too. Even when he's near as the end of your nose, people make like he's nowhere around. They won't talk to him. They won't listen to him. They keep their eye on the ground. But here in this place there's no strangers, and Jesus, he isn't a stranger either. The Kingdom of Heaven's like this."

He said, "We all got secrets. I got them same as everybody else— things we feel bad about and wish hadn't ever happened. Hurtful things. We're all scared and lonesome, but most of the time we keep it hid. It's like every one of us has lost his way so bad we don't even know which way is home any more only we're ashamed to ask. You know what would happen if we would own up we're lost and ask? Why, what would happen is we'd find home is each other. We'd find out home is Jesus loves us lost or found or any whichway."[7]

It is easy to imagine that the table talk at the meals described by Luke radiated just this sort of poignancy and power.

As we conclude our overview of Luke's focus on hospitality, we should give some attention to the frequent and sometimes subtle reversals that occur in the guest and host roles played by our author's chief characters. Above all, this fluidity applies to Jesus. We have already noted that in Luke's Gospel the picture of Jesus as wanderer has been developed more consistently than in the other two Synoptics. Thus, on one level, Luke's Jesus always enters upon the scene as a guest in need of hospitality. He has nowhere to lay his head (9:58), unless a kind host obliges. Indeed, Luke alone gives us the impression that Jesus often spent his nights out in the open (6:12; 9:28–37; 21:37).[8] But on another level this man without a home is obviously the supreme host, the welcomer par excellence to God's kingdom. At the home of Simon the Pharisee, for example, Jesus first appears in the role of guest. But as the story moves forward, he is the one who takes charge and hosts the occasion, first by teaching Simon a lesson and then by declaring God's forgiveness to the sinful woman who has anointed his feet. To both he opens the door to new life (7:35–50). For similar role reversals in Luke's story of Jesus see 5:29–39; 10:38–42; 11:27–28; 14:1–24; 19:1–27; 24:13–35. In each of these accounts Jesus the guest extends some form of invitation to his hosts or table partners. All but the first passage are unique to the Third Gospel.

As if to summarize the ministry of Jesus, Luke reports: "Now the tax collectors and sinners were all drawing near to hear him. And the Pharisees and scribes murmured, saying, 'This man receives sinners and eats with them'" (15:1–2). The marginal messiah welcomes other marginal people. He is God's traveling householder *(oikodespotēs)*, inviting every Israelite to the banquet of the kingdom (14:16–24), but in the end admitting only those who repent (13:24–30; 23:43).

In Acts Peter and Paul sometimes shift their roles from guest to host (10:1–48; 20:7–12, 27–33); even as a prisoner Paul can exercise the host's function (16:25–32; 27:21–36; 28:17, 30–31). Nevertheless, he differs from Jesus in that he is never a thoroughgoing itinerant. With Paul, the picture that emerges is of one who has the capability of taking up the position of residential leader (13:1) and paying his own expenses (18:1–3; 20:33–35; 28:30–31). In other words, the central missionary figure in Acts is less dependent than Jesus upon the hospitality of others. As a matter of fact, Luke often seems to recount the offerings of hospitality to apostles primarily in order to praise the respective hosts for their virtue (see, e.g., 12:12; 16:14–15, 40; 17:5–9, 10–11; 18:1–3, 7; 21:4–6, 8–10, 15–17; 27:1–3; 28:2–10, 13–14). As our investigation moves forward, we shall want to ask ourselves why Luke preserves so many of these brief encounters in his second volume.

TO HONOR THE WANDERING PROPHETS

All four evangelists portray Jesus as a prophet, though in such a way as to show that this title, by itself, does not suffice to explain his identity. That is, Jesus speaks and acts prophetically within his higher office of messiah. However, when Luke is measured against his three colleagues, he, far more than the others, allows Jesus' prophetic role to *shape* his messiahship. This tendency appears most clearly in the gospel material that only Luke records, and in two passages from Acts.

Within the Third Gospel our author's unique material is usually called "special Luke" (SL). Some of this has found its way to him in the form of oral or written sources, and some of it results from his own editorial shaping of the various traditions he has chosen to employ. Below are the main examples of SL in which Jesus' prophetic identity comes to the foreground:

Special Luke

4:25–27	Jesus compares his ministry to that of Elijah and Elisha.
6:8	Jesus reads the thoughts of his opponents with prophetic insight (see also 7:40–50).
6:17–49	Jesus comes down from a mountain to proclaim God's word to the people, just as Moses did in Exod. 34:29.
7:11–17	Jesus raises the dead son of the widow of Nain in a narrative based upon Elijah's similar feat. In fact, 7:15 is a direct quote from the Elijah story (1 Kings 17:23).
7:39	Simon the Pharisee's words of reproach ("If this man were a prophet, he would have known . . .") are shown by the rest of the story to be ironic. The reader learns that Jesus *does* know; therefore he *is* a prophet.
10:1–24	Jesus selects seventy helpers, just as Moses did in Num. 11:24–25.
13:33	Concerning his ministry, Jesus remarks: "I must go on my way today and tomorrow and the day following; for it cannot be that a prophet should perish away from Jerusalem."
24:19	On their way to Emmaus two of Jesus' disciples inform the stranger who accompanies them that their crucified master was "a prophet mighty in deed and word."

To this data may be added C. F. Evans's observation regarding the Lukan travel narrative (9:51—19:28):

> The conclusion is difficult to resist that the evangelist has selected and arranged his material in such a way as to present it in a Deuteronomic sequence. His motive for doing so is not far to seek; it will have sprung from the conviction . . . that Jesus was the prophet like unto Moses.[9]

This same Lukan conviction surfaces in Acts 3:22, where Peter quotes Deut. 18:15 ("The Lord God will raise up for you a prophet from your brethren as he raised me [Moses] up") with reference to Jesus.

In a similar manner the speech of Stephen functions to depict the life of Moses so as to draw a direct line of continuity between him and Jesus (see esp. 7:37).

When we set the results of this short study alongside those of our first section, a clear picture emerges. Luke wants his readers to think of Jesus as a *wandering prophet messiah*. Not only is he the heir and fulfillment of all those great figures from Israel's past who have called it to repentance; he is also the eschatological traveler who crisscrosses the land, making sure that everyone has the opportunity to hear God's gracious invitation (Luke 4:14, 43–44; Acts 10:38).

But why does Luke construct his story of Jesus in this way? In a recent monograph Richard Dillon points toward a plausible answer. By means of source and form analysis Dillon shows that in a good number of cases the core parts of the SL material dealing with hospitality are traditional, that is, inherited by our author instead of being shaped or created by him. This phenomenon occurs most strikingly in the story of the sinful woman's anointing of Jesus' feet, where hospitality concerns are explicitly linked with an emphasis upon Jesus' prophetic identity (7:36–50). But similar combinations at the level of tradition also turn up in the banquet scene "at the house of a ruler who belonged to the Pharisees" (14:1–24) and in the Samaritan narratives, which include the parable of the good Samaritan (10:29–37), as well as an account of inhospitality toward Jesus and his disciples on the part of a Samaritan village (9:51–56).[10] Likewise, the parable of the prodigal son and the narratives concerning Mary and Martha and Zaccheus are best understood as pre-Lukan and in any event are compatible with the guest-host themes transmitted by those who supplied Luke with his distinctive sources. Indeed, Dillon proposes that Luke's version of Q, which itself contains quite a number of prophet-guest-host combinations (e.g., 4:23–30; 7:31–35; 9:57–62; 10:4–16; 11:37–52; 13:22–30), came to him from this same group of people.[11]

But now the question arises: Why did Luke's predecessors shape their material as they did? And further, why was Luke sympathetic to their concerns? At this point Dillon draws upon the groundbreaking word of Gerd Theissen to argue that those who formed Luke's mind with their life and teaching were "wandering charismatics," that is, early missionary prophets who followed Jesus' itinerant life style quite literally and with great rigor. For these prophets, only someone who had renounced all things—home, family, and possessions—could claim to be a true disciple of Jesus (14:33, which is unique to Luke). The mission command to "carry no purse, no bag, no sandals" (10:4) was understood by them as a lifelong program. Being careful to distinguish themselves from beggars ("salute no one on the road . . . do not go from house to house"; 10:4b, 7b), they nevertheless depended for their material needs upon those who responded with hospitality to their healing power and preaching of the kingdom (10:5–11).[12]

Dillon contends that many of the stories and sayings in Luke's version of Q, as well as the bulk of SL, are best interpreted as a kind of propaganda literature which supports the teachings and goals of these wandering prophets. Thus, the Mary and Martha pericope shows that "there was not to be so much care lavished on the accommodation of the traveler that his words of instruction could not be attended to."[13] In a similar manner, the story of the sinful woman at Simon's house relates the experience of the prophets that "their own accommodations had probably to be found most often amongst people like the repentant woman, whereas citizens of stature offered them scant welcome."[14] According to Dillon, Luke's special tradition again and again makes the point that society's outcasts would serve as the best hosts to God's messengers because they, more than others, were ready to accept Jesus' banquet invitation (now issued through the words and acts of his wandering followers).

There can be little doubt that such traveling missionaries actually existed or that they played a substantial role in the life of the early church.[15] Although neither Dillon nor Theissen suggests it, we may speculate that Luke himself spent some time in their company. At any rate, it is clear that he honors the witness of their life and work by passing along to his readers more traditions stamped with their character than any other New Testament writer. For Luke, as well as those who helped to shape his story of Jesus, there was something lastingly authentic about the way of the wandering prophet. Thus he could not compose his gospel without clothing it in the memories and self-understandings of the itinerants.

TO ENCOURAGE THE
RESIDENT PROPHETS

Nevertheless, a number of anomalies remain as we try to describe the full meaning of hospitality in Luke's two-volume work. Chief among these is the fact that in Acts few of the convictions and ideals espoused by the wandering prophets survive. It is no longer the poor and outcast, or those relying upon their welcome, who occupy center stage. Instead, the individuals who attain prominence in Luke's story of the early church consist primarily of residential leaders (starting with the Jerusalem apostles), travelers sent out from residential "home bases," and the mostly middle and upper class people who accept them into their households. To this shift in our author's focus we must add Theissen's provocative observation that "Luke fought in his own time the descendants of the first itinerant charismatics who were from his point of view false prophets."[16] If Theissen's contention applies primarily to Acts, it is understandable. But why then would Luke take so much care in the Gospel to preserve and lift up values that are largely omitted from his second volume?

An examination of the term "prophet" will help us take the first step toward resolving this difficulty. Although Luke presents Jesus as the messianic prophet without equal and shows, by his use of their sources, that he honors the early missionaries who have adopted Jesus' itinerant manner of life, he nevertheless makes clear, already in the Third Gospel, that he will not allow these charismatic figures to claim the title of prophet exclusively for themselves. Using the words of John the Baptist, Luke assures his readers that Jesus will someday baptize *all* his followers with the Holy Spirit (3:16), thus equipping each one of them for the prophetic role. This democratization of prophecy is also previewed in Jesus' appointment of the seventy (10:1–20; unique to Luke's version of Q), a story that parallels the Old Testament account of God's reapportioning to seventy of Israel's elders the spirit of prophetic wisdom that had heretofore resided only upon Moses (Num. 11:16–25). This narrative is followed by Moses' words of hope that "all of the Lord's people [would be] prophets, that the Lord would put his spirit upon them" (Num. 11:29). Finally, in a postresurrection speech of Jesus which Luke alone records, the disciples are promised that all of them (a large number according to 24:33) will be "clothed with power from on high" (24:49). Here Luke sets the stage for Pentecost, where about 120 followers of Jesus are visited by the mighty rushing wind and tongues of fire that enable them to proclaim God's mighty acts in many languages (Acts 2:11). To help his readers understand the extraordinary breadth of this outpouring, Luke has Peter interpret it with the words of the prophet Joel:

> And in the last days it shall be, God declares, that I will pour out my Spirit upon all flesh, and your sons and your daughters shall prophesy, and your young men shall see visions, and your old men shall dream dreams; yea, and on my menservants and my maidservants in those days I will pour out my Spirit; and they shall prophesy. (Acts 2:17–18)

Luke adds the last words "and they shall prophesy" to the Old Testament text, probably to emphasize once again that everyone will be ennobled by this gift of the Spirit. Even those on the lowest rungs of society's ladder will speak prophetically in this dawning of the new age. What Moses longed for is now coming to pass.

To be sure, Luke does not apply the term "prophet" to every Christian in Acts. But the data just presented seems to justify Minear's contention that our author wishes to advocate some form of "prophethood of all believers."[17] Presumably Luke is observing the Pauline distinction between those who prophesy regularly, thereby assuming the office of prophet in a given place (1 Cor. 12:27–29), and the congregation as a whole, which is urged "earnestly [to] desire the spiritual gifts, especially that you prophesy" (14:1; see also vv. 24, 31).

But we need to say more about how the term "prophet" as such functions in Acts. If in the Third Gospel the noun applies chiefly to Israel's past prophets, to John and Jesus, and, by implication, to the wandering followers of Jesus in the early church who have renounced all claims to home, family, and possessions, a strikingly different understanding prevails in Acts. There we discover that every single individual named as a prophet—and every occasional prophesier as well—is assumed to be a member of a residential congregation. Below is an overview of the evidence:

Acts

2:1–4   The 120 members of the nascent church in Jerusalem prophesy as they are filled with the Spirit.

11:27–30   Prophets from the Jerusalem congregation come down
             to the church at Antioch for a visit. Among them is
             Agabus, who foresees a great famine.

13:1–3   The resident "prophets and teachers" of the church at
             Antioch are identified as Barnabas, Simeon Niger,
             Lucius of Cyrene, Manaen, and Saul, later to become
             Paul.

15:32–35   Judas and Silas, two members of the church in Jerusa-
             lem, "who were themselves prophets," accompany
             Barnabas and Paul back to Antioch for the purpose of
             exhorting believers there to accept the newly formu-
             lated apostolic decree.

19:1–7   About a dozen followers of John the Baptist, who
             reside in Ephesus, receive the Holy Spirit through the
             hands of Paul, with the result that they "spoke with
             tongues and prophesied."

21:8–9   The four unmarried daughters of Philip the evangelist
             prophesy at his home in Caesarea.

21:10   Agabus of Jerusalem (see 1:27–30) appears at Philip's
             house to foretell Paul's imminent imprisonment (see
             also 21:4).

To this picture we may add a few more details. Although the two
Hellenists, Stephen and Philip (6:5—8:40), are never called prophets,
Luke clearly wants his readers to view their work as prophetic in
character (see esp. chap. 7). Stephen remains a resident of Jerusalem
throughout his Spirit-filled career. Philip flees the city because of the
persecution that follows Stephen's death and becomes a traveling
evangelist. But his itinerant life is quite temporary. Precisely as
evangelist, he is led by the Spirit to settle down in Caesarea. There he
becomes a householder and fathers, or is reunited with, a family
(8:40; 21:8–14). In a similar manner the eloquent teacher of Scripture
Apollos is portrayed chiefly as a resident. Instructed by Priscilla and
Aquila during his stay in Ephesus, he then moves on to Corinth.
There he is accepted into the congregation by virtue of a recommen-
dation written for him by his Ephesian hosts (18:24—19:1).

     From this type of shaping on our author's part we might indeed
draw Theissen's conclusion, namely, that Luke is "fighting" the de-

scendants of the first itinerant charismatics because he considers them to be false prophets. Taken as a unity, however, Luke-Acts is hardly a polemical document.[18] Moreover, we have already noted that in his Gospel Luke takes pains to honor the lives and values of the itinerants for his readers. Is it then a matter of displacement by stages? Is Luke saying that the wandering prophets have served their purpose magnificently (the Third Gospel), but that now, in the closing decades of the first century, resident prophets must take up the mantle of leadership and become the church's prime authorities (Acts)?[19]

Although such an interpretation would help to explain some of the data in Luke-Acts, it does not do justice to the whole sweep of the work. It seems more likely that Luke's composition is aimed at building up local leadership so that it can strengthen the whole church *for partnership with the wandering prophets*. Thus, Luke alone among the writers of the New Testament explicitly calls residential believers "disciples" (Acts 6:1–7; 9:1–38; 11:26–30, etc.) and refers to their community life as "the Way" (9:2; 19:9, 23; 22:4). The effect of this terminology is to give residential Christianity a pilgrimage quality, though without simply declaring the wandering prophets to be inauthentic or obsolete. Indeed, Luke appears to be sketching out a future for the church in which all parties can play a vital role. In this respect he may be properly called a "catholic" writer. As we shall see, a number of passages, even in the Gospel, serve to enhance the relationship between wanderers and residents.[20] To the degree that Luke addresses the strict itinerants or their supporters per se, he is asking them to become more residential than they have been, to lend their talents more humbly and graciously to local communities, and to share leadership in missionary ventures with believers in households and families, who cannot travel great distances to proclaim the gospel. It is to this second group, the residential disciples, and especially their leaders, that Luke directs the bulk of his two-volume work. They are to think of themselves as colleagues with the first noble imitators of Jesus, co-workers in a grand missionary alliance.

One way in which Luke imparts this message is through his rendition of Paul's career in Acts. If the residential readers of Luke-Acts have tended to think of the martyred Paul and his associate Barnabas as professional wanderers, exalted figures quite different from themselves and far removed from their own domestic concerns (a knowledge of Paul's letters among these readers is not presupposed), then our author is out to change that understanding. Indeed, Luke attempts nothing less than the residentialization of the great traveler Paul, and he does this in order to help his readers see themselves as legitimate heirs of the heroic apostle.

Thus, it becomes important for Luke's readers to see that Paul's history as a believer begins with the residential disciple Ananias and the community at Damascus to which he belongs. Without this local church's courageous welcoming of its persecutor, there would have been no Christian Paul. Furthermore, Paul's career as a missionary first blossoms, humanly speaking, only when the residential believer Barnabas ventures beyond the fear of his associates that Paul might be a secret agent of the Jerusalem authorities and recommends him to the apostles (9:26-30). In the language of hospitality, Barnabas welcomes the fringe Christian Paul into the mainstream of the church's life. When this volatile newcomer proceeds to make himself just as unpopular in Jerusalem as he had been in Damascus and must retreat to his home in Tarsus to escape assassination (9:28-30), Barnabas once again takes up his cause. Having visited the frontier church in Antioch, where Jews and Gentiles are worshiping together for the first time, Barnabas sees an opportunity for himself and Paul to work side by side among its leaders:

> So Barnabas traveled out to Tarsus to search for Saul [Paul]; and when he had found him, he brought him to Antioch. And thus it happened that they joined forces for an entire year in the church and taught a great number of people. (11:25-26; au. trans.)

With this story Luke establishes that Paul and Barnabas themselves assumed the role of resident teachers (and prophets; 13:1) in the church of Antioch long before they became traveling missionaries. Indeed, Paul never really gives up this role, for even as an itinerant he remains an agent, that is, "apostle" (14:4, 14) of Antioch, with this great church as his home base (13:2-3; 14:26; 15:35; 18:22-23).

The point Luke makes for his readers then is that the legendary traveler Paul is actually a resident at heart. This note receives amplification in Luke's detailed coverage of Paul's long-term stays in the major urban congregations of Asia Minor and Europe. Thus, the apostle from Antioch is said to have lived more than a year and a half in Corinth (18:11, 18), two years and three months in Ephesus (19:8–10), and "two whole years" under house arrest in Rome, where he "welcomed all who came to him preaching the kingdom of God and teaching about the Lord Jesus Christ quite openly and unhindered" (28:30–31). Inasmuch as this last report serves to conclude the Book of Acts, we must suspect that it provides a kind of summary statement of what Luke is up to. In essence, he wants his residential readers to be guided by the life and work of Paul, who was both one of themselves and a wanderer at the same time. The nature of Luke's counsel to his readers via the career of Paul will be explored below.

But first we need to review the Third Gospel from the vantage point of what we have learned about our author's purposes in Acts. Let us try out the hypothesis that even as he tells his story of the homeless prophet Jesus, thereby honoring the charismatic itinerants who became Jesus' first imitators, Luke is already at work instructing his target audience of residential believers in the privileges and responsibilities that they are to share with their traveling colleagues. If substantial parts of the Gospel make sense on this redactional reading, we may consider our hypothesis to be well founded.

In his article, "Poor and Rich: The Lukan Sitz im Leben," Robert Karris shows that the numerous passages in our Third Gospel that deal with possessions are mostly directed to those who have them, not to the poor or to those who have already renounced their earthly goods.[21] Thus, Jesus' disciples (on our hypothesis, the primarily residential readers of the Gospel) are bidden to "give to everyone who begs from you . . . lend, expecting nothing in return"(6:30, 35) and "sell your possessions [in order to] give alms" (12:33). That Luke does not want his readers to think of a single, once-for-all selling and giving is made clear in 14:33, where the command to divest occurs in the present tense—the best translation would be: "whoever of you does not continue to renounce all that he has cannot be my disciple"—and forms the capstone for two short parables of Jesus which emphasize perseverance and prudence in the use of resources (14:28–32). All of this material is distinctive to the Third Gospel.

To underscore his intent, Luke describes the rich ruler, who has asked Jesus what he must do to inherit eternal life, as one who stands by sadly when he hears the command to sell everything he has and "distribute to the poor" (18:18–23).[22] The picture is one of suspense (will he or won't he?) and is probably meant to provide sober counsel for well-to-do members of the Christian communities to which Luke writes. We may detect a similar thrust in the Zaccheus story (19:1–10), although here the exemplary host is not asked to sell everything. For Luke, a variety of authentic responses to Jesus' call is possible. Indeed, the message given to believers of means in Luke's parable of the pounds, which follows directly upon his account of Zaccheus (19:11–27), is that they are to "trade" with their goods, presumably by investing them in the church's mission so that a spiritual-material profit will result (18:30).[23] "Everyone to whom much is given, of him will much be required" (12:48). Here again, the idea is that this distribution should be done prudently over a long period of time. Residential believers are not asked to impoverish themselves.

Leaders especially are portrayed in the role of the "wise steward" *(oikonomos)* who gives all household dependents "their portion of food at the proper time" (12:42).[24] If the steward (residential host) executes his task faithfully, the master (Christ) will come and "set him over all his possessions" (12:44). This probably refers to a future reward, but Luke elsewhere assures his residential readers that even now their purse for almsgiving will be replenished from a heavenly treasury (12:33). We may surmise that at the redactional level the parable of the dishonest steward (16:1–13), the story of Martha and Mary (10:38–42), and a number of sayings by Jesus concerning householders (11:5–13; 12:35–40; 14:12–24; 22:11)—all of which are unique to Luke's Gospel or heavily shaped by his editorial hand—likewise serve to instruct residential believers. This would also hold true for the negative examples of the rich fool, who hoards his wealth instead of distributing it (12:16–21), and the prosperous man who denies Lazarus even the crumbs from his table (16:19–31).

Thus, already in Luke's Gospel Jesus offers instructions for those who will follow his Way within the framework of families and local congregations. His authority over the life of the home derives from the fact that he, the archetypal wanderer, is also God's chief householder (13:25–30; 14:21–24; 23:42–43). His kingdom, the church, is like a table, that is, a physical place to which those hungering and thirsting for salvation can come (15:1–2; 22:30). At this table Jesus both presides (12:42–48; 24:30) and serves as a waiter (22:25–27).

Therefore, his residential disciples, beginning with the Twelve, must do likewise (12:42–53; 22:27–30).

A significant elaboration upon this teaching occurs in 17:7–10, a parable of Jesus that only Luke records. Addressed to "the apostles" (v. 5), it goes as follows:

> (7) Will any one of you, who has a servant *(doulos)* plowing or keeping sheep, say to him when he has come in from the field, "Come at once and sit down at table?" (8) Will he not rather say to him, "Prepare supper for me, and gird yourself and serve me, till I eat and drink; and afterward you shall eat and drink?" (9) Does he thank the servant because he did what was commanded? (10) So you also, when you have done all that is commanded, say, "We are unworthy servants; we have only done what was our duty."

Minear has pointed out that this parable lists three "apostolic" activities: plowing, in the sense of spreading the word; shepherding or leading; and serving at table. The first two are done in the field, probably as forms of itinerant ministry.[25] But the third activity must be associated with a residence, a place to which the field workers come for rest from their labors. In Luke's purview Jesus would be speaking to itinerant believers who think they have a right to be served by residential believers.

But now comes a surprise. The itinerants are told that they should not expect to sit at ease in the household but that they must serve their master also as waiters. Minear concludes from this turn of events that Luke is here speaking to a "distinction between field work and housework [which] was the source of conflict among the apostles in the post-Easter church."[26] This view coheres with our hypothesis, but we can also say more. In v. 10, which may be Luke's own addition to the parable, we learn that there is really only one ministry ("all that is commanded"). If itinerants must serve at tables, then, by implication, residents may become missionaries and leaders. For Luke, the three-fold apostolic work is capable of division between wanderers and local congregations in a variety of ways. But neither group can claim superiority over the other. All servants are so far below their master that they must call themselves "unworthy." For this reason they must always remain humble and obedient, taking care to serve one another, just as Jesus did (22:27). Since the parable is addressed to itinerants, the effect of the whole is to raise the status of the people whom they regard as underlings. Here then Luke seems to be taking the part of residential believers over against those in the church of his day who think that their permanent renunciation of a fixed home confers upon them (and them alone) the rank of true discipleship.[27]

The "apostles" with whom Luke takes issue are not the Twelve, who appear in Acts as residential believers (e.g., 8:1), but wandering prophets like those referred to in *Didache* 11:4–6:

> Let every apostle who comes to you be received as the Lord, but let him not stay more than one day, or if need be a second as well; but if he stay three days he is a false prophet. And when an apostle goes forth let him accept nothing but bread till he reach his night's lodging; but if he ask for money, he is a false prophet.

In these situations the term "apostle" is probably a self-designation, more or less equivalent to "authoritative prophet-teacher" (see Did. 11:7–10; 13:1–7, and n. 15 in this chapter). It does not denote one who comes as an emissary of a particular congregation.

By way of summary, we have been proposing that not only in Acts but also in his Gospel Luke makes a special effort to address residential believers. He does this in order to affirm their roles as genuine ministers of the word (Luke 1:2) and to instruct them in the details of their vocation. Sometimes he explicitly names these residents as prophets. Always he assumes their prophetic character (see esp. Luke 11:13; 21:13–15; Acts 2:17–18). Luke does not contest the authenticity of the itinerant ministers who have contributed so much to the church's mission, only their claims to superiority. In fact, our author presses for a partnership in ministry by means of which both wanderers and residents, who may be estranged from one another, can join forces to advance the gospel. We turn now to an examination of that partnership.

TOWARD A COOPERATIVE
HOUSE CHURCH MISSION

To a modern reader, Luke seems virtually obsessed with houses and other civic or cultic structures. It has often been noted that his story of Jesus essentially begins and ends in the Jerusalem temple (Luke 1:5–23; 24:53). What has not been so frequently stressed is that Acts begins and ends in a residential dwelling (1:4, 13; 2:1; 28:23, 30–

31). Moreover, Lukan additions of the terms for "house" (usually *oikos* or *oikia*) to the Q source and the Markan outline number roughly twenty-eight. Some of these may have been in the tradition Luke inherited, and some of them are metaphorical usages that do not depict actual dwellings (e.g., 1:27, 69; 13:35). On the whole, however, the evidence suggests that our author himself has inserted most of the references. Indeed, for him, residential buildings take on a kind of spiritual significance. Some notable examples follow:

Mary praises God with her *Magnificat* in the house of Zechariah and Elizabeth, where she has found refuge from gossip and ostracism in the early stages of her pregnancy (1:39–56).

Levi's house becomes the locale for a "great feast" which the converted toll collector gives to honor his new master Jesus (5:29; contrast Matt. 9:10 and Mark 2:15, where the place and purpose of the meal are unclear).

Luke's Gerasene demoniac is shown to be suffering severe deprivation in that "he lived not in a house but among the tombs" (8:27). Thus, for our author, the demoniac's homecoming (8:39) becomes a central feature of his healing.

Luke's version of the great feast has Jesus telling his hearers: "Go out to the highways and hedges and compel people to come in that my house (contrast Matthew's 'wedding hall') may be filled" (14:23). While Matthew's rendition of Q portrays the final judgment, Luke's parallel account describes the church's mission.

Houses function as indispensable stages for the Lukan dramas of Mary and Martha, Jesus' meals with Pharisees, the woman who loses and finds a coin, the prodigal son, the rich man and Lazarus, and Zaccheus.

Luke alone reports that the first trial of Jesus took place in the high priest's house (22:54).

When we turn to Acts, it becomes immediately obvious that

houses, synagogues (some of which were probably houses), temples, and other public structures play a huge role in the development of the early church's mission. Luke's account of Pentecost sets the theme, for here the real Actor of Acts, the Holy Spirit, creates the church in a private dwelling (2:1–4).[28] Born in a house, the missionary venture proceeds outward; yet it never forsakes its place of origin (2:46). Although some houses belonging to believers are later sold (4:34–35), this seems to happen only when the need for funds arises.[29] Other believers, like Mary the mother of Mark, retain their properties in Jerusalem and place them at the church's disposal as meeting places (12:12–17).

Here we do well to pause for a moment and incorporate this general impression of Acts, along with the distinctive references to houses in Luke's Gospel, into the framework of our overall hypothesis. If, as we have been arguing, Luke wants to address residential believers, especially those with some wealth and influence, then our author's great interest in dwellings should be translated into an emphatic affirmation of house church Christianity, the kind his readers know best. For Luke, it is not only the road traveled by the wandering prophets but also, and perhaps even more, the household of believers where the Way of God unfolds.

How, specifically, does this happen? We have already noted above how frequently, in both the Third Gospel and Acts, God's messengers receive food and/or lodging from those to whom they minister. There is much evidence to suggest that Luke never thinks of these encounters as simple material transactions, even when they are mentioned only in passing. On the contrary, our author intends for his readers to consider such meetings pregnant occasions for God's reciprocity, quantum leaps in the progress of the gospel through gift exchanges among humans. Thus, we find that especially in Luke's references to houses and house churches the central features of Christian community life come into view. These include the proclamation of the gospel (Luke 8:39; 10:5–8; Acts 2:14–36; 5:42; 10:34–43; 18:7–17; 19:9; 21:8;[30] 28:30–31); teaching (Luke 7:36–50; 10:38–42; 11:37–52; 14:1–24; 22:24–38; Acts 2:42; 5:42; 18:11, 26; 20:9, 20; 28:30–31); acts of worship and liturgy such as prayer, praise, fasting, baptism, and the Lord's Supper (Luke 1:46–55; 22:14–23; 24:28–35; Acts 1:14; 2:46–47; 4:23–30; 9:10–22; 10:1–8; 12:12; 13:2; 16:33; 20:7–12);

healing (Luke 4:38–41; 5:18–26; 7:10; 10:5–9; Acts 9:17–18, 36–43; 19:16; 20:9–12; 28:8); prophecy (Acts 2:1–21; 15:32–33; 21:4, 10–14); revelations and visions (Luke 24:29–35; Acts 1:13–26; 9:10–19; 10:3–8, 9–23; 11:13–14; 13:2; 18:9–10; 23:11); the distribution of goods to the needy (Luke 12:42; 19:1–10; Acts 2:45; 4:34–37; 6:1–6; 9:36–43; 20:34–35); and the provision of refuge for those living in hostile environments (Luke 1:39–55; 10:30–37; 16:4–5; Acts 12:12–17; 17:5–9; 18:7).

Our brief schematic overview cannot begin to convey the richness of these stories. Readers who take the time to look up just a few of the references cited above will soon come to appreciate the consummate skill with which Luke has presented the house church as the creative hub of God's redemptive work. By and large, the residential communities described are lively and winsome ones, filled with the Spirit and ready for adventure. Above all, these churches are banquet communities, celebrating the abundance of God in Christ which is continually opening up doors for repentance. By virtue of their lived faith members of the house church congregations quite naturally "invite" their neighbors to travel God's Way along with them:

> And day by day, attending the temple together and breaking bread in their homes, they partook of food with glad and generous hearts, praising God and having favor with all the people. And the Lord added to their number day by day those who were being saved. (Acts 2:46–47)

The Bolivian theologian Mortimer Arias has recently characterized this attractive quality of life as "centripetal mission or evangelization by hospitality." Moreover, he has argued that today we need to take it far more seriously than we do in our proclamation of the gospel.[31]

Already in the first century the stories recorded in Luke-Acts must have functioned as encouragements to residential believers. Like the heroes and heroines of Luke's two-volume panorama they were being called to take their places at the very center of the divine mission. Their own small churches, which may have seemed to them quite an insignificant force in the world of their day, were being extolled as God's chief instrument for outreach to the nations. In Luke's view, the house church represented a providential place of opportunity. Thus, in the closing verses of Acts, he shows that despite Paul's confinement to rented quarters, his missionary work proceeded with great success:

> And he lived there two whole years at his own expense, and welcomed
> all who came to him, preaching the kingdom of God and teaching about
> the Lord Jesus Christ quite openly and unhindered. (Acts 28:30–31)

The phrase "quite openly and unhindered," which also constitutes
the last portion of the Greek text of Acts and should therefore be
taken as emphatic, suggests a conviction on Luke's part that house
churches will henceforth be the most promising of all social institutions for the proclamation of the gospel.[32] Yet these words do not
signify freedom from persecution. Luke's addressees know that Paul
has suffered a martyr's death (Acts 20:25, 38) and that the same fate
may befall them (Luke 21:12–17). Nevertheless, having read Luke-
Acts, they also know how wondrously God can use small communities of believers to turn the world upside down (Acts 17:6–34). The
mission of the house churches is to take up their part in this continuing transformation.[33]

But why should we call such a mission "cooperative"? We do so
because Luke, in arranging his material, clearly makes special efforts
to promote harmonious relationships between itinerants and residents for the sake of their common work. While his main interest is in
supporting and encouraging the prophetic ministry of residential
believers (see above, especially our treatment of Luke 17:7–10), he
does not simply forget about the contributions of the itinerants or
declare their missionary efforts obsolete. Nor does he deny them an
important share in the ongoing leadership of the church. Rather, what
we find in Luke's two-volume work, particularly in Acts, is an attempt
on his part to provide models for flexibility with regard to ministerial
roles. Neither itinerants nor residents can define themselves too
exclusively in terms of the activities they have come to regard as
specific to their manner of life (guest, host, leader, servant, giver,
receiver, minister of the word, minister of tables, etc.). It is the nature
of God's Spirit always to challenge the self-images of believers so that
the gospel may advance.

Luke would have appreciated the modern variant on this theme
that surfaces in a story about Will Campbell, the back road preacher
and civil rights activist of the sixties who has lately taken to visiting
members of the Ku Klux Klan in their homes:

> Asked by one Atlanta churchman, "You think you're ever going to save

the souls of the KKK?," Campbell replied, "Naw, this business of saving souls sometimes works in peculiar ways. Maybe they'll save *my* soul. At the least, I can always count on them asking me to play my guitar."[34]

For Luke as well as Will Campbell, a cooperative mission, a mutual ministry characterized by surprising role reversals, lies at the heart of God's plan.

We may cite further examples from Acts to flesh out this observation. In general, we can say that the itinerants Luke chooses to portray move toward long-term sharing relationships with local congregations. They are called out from such communities (Acts 11:23; 13:1-3, 5; 16:1-5) and tend to settle down in them for months and years at a time (12:17; 14:27-28; 18:11, 22-23, 27-28; 19:8-10; 20:31). On one level Paul, the central figure in Acts, corresponds to the model of the wandering charismatic. Led by the Spirit (16:7-10, 19-21), he and his associates crisscross the trade routes of Asia Minor and southeastern Europe preaching the gospel, teaching, and healing. On numerous occasions they accept food and lodging from those who come to faith through their words. But Luke wants his readers to see that the story of mission is far more complex than this. Luke's Paul is no free agent of an unmediated Spirit; nor is he fundamentally dependent upon the hospitality of his hearers. This Paul is the apostle from Antioch. There he experiences the Spirit's call to missionary work. From there he is sent out by his residential cobelievers with a laying on of hands and (probably) money for his journey (13:1-3). To Antioch Paul returns, reporting on his labors and reacquainting himself with his home base (14:26-28; 15:30-35; 18:22-23).

Moreover, during his extended residences in Corinth and Ephesus—to which Luke devotes practically three chapters—Paul forms missionary partnerships with local believers which depart from the standard practice of payment in food and lodging for spiritual services rendered. While living in Corinth, Paul stays at the home of Priscilla and Aquila and labors with them at the tentmaker's craft (18:1-3). This is no simple matter of extending hospitality to a traveling authority figure. Presumably the home workshop was a center for missionary activity in which all three believers participated. Thus, when Paul leaves Corinth, his friends accompany him as far as Ephesus and take up their own mission work in the local synagogue (18:24-28). Here then is a story about cooperation between itinerants and residents (amplified in Rom. 16:3-4). As for Paul's three-year residence in Ephesus, he does indeed act as an authority figure who teaches the local elders. But he is not a visiting charismatic who trades his wisdom for room and board. It would be better to call him a "first among equals" who earns his authority over a long period of time by means of his exemplary life in Ephesus (see esp. Acts 19). This Paul is no drain on the financial resources of the residential believers among whom he lives. As he bids farewell to his Ephesian friends, he reminds them of his stewardship:

> You yourselves know how I lived among you all the time from the first day I set foot in Asia, serving the Lord in all humility and with tears and with trials which befell me through the plots of the Jews; how I did not shrink from declaring to you anything that was profitable, and teaching you in public from house to house. . . . Therefore be alert, remembering that for three years I did not cease night or day to admonish everyone with tears. . . . I coveted no one's silver or gold or apparel. You yourselves know that these hands ministered to my necessities, and to those who were with me. In all things I have shown you that by so toiling one must help the weak, remembering the words of the Lord Jesus, how he said, "It is more blessed to give than to receive." (20:18-35)

Here the last few sentences serve as an encouragement for residential leaders to carry on the mission of the church among their neighbors by means of generous giving. Once again we may detect what Arias has called "centripetal mission." When nonbelievers in Ephesus see how well the local church nurtures its own people, they will feel themselves drawn to its teachings.

In summary, we may say that Luke uses stories about Paul to impress upon his readers the fluidity of the missionary task. Paul is both itinerant and resident, guest and host, minister of the word and minister of the table. As such, he becomes a prime example for all believers, but particularly for the residents Luke wishes to address. This does not mean that every believer will play all roles, but it does mean that each one must anticipate the Spirit's call to shift roles for the sake of the gospel. Indeed, there is considerable evidence in Luke-Acts that our author expects some of his residential readers to adopt an itinerant missionary life, at least for a while.[35]

Finally, however, we recall the one role that must be taken up and never relinquished by all who aspire to maturity in the Way. At the last supper Luke's Jesus gives these instructions to his disciples:

The kings of the Gentiles exercise lordship over them; and those in authority over them are called benefactors. But not so with you; rather let the greatest among you become as the youngest, and the leader as one who serves. For which is greater, one who sits at table, or one who serves? Is it not the one who sits at table? But I am among you as one who serves. (Luke 22:25–27)

Only as believers persist in serving one another with such humility, establishing their authority as a shared one, from the bottom up, can residents and itinerants achieve harmonious relationships. It is this corporate authority, emerging most graphically in the daily life of the house church, that empowers believers for cooperative mission.

MISSION AS
SPIRITUAL-MATERIAL WELCOMING

The mission of the house churches is conceived of by Luke in quite holistic terms. For him, all those on the outside of the redemptive community must be invited in so that both their bodies and their spirits can experience God's refreshment (Acts 3:19). Accordingly, Luke takes care to point up the essential unity between ministries of the word and ministries of the table. The historical Jesus/risen Christ (Luke 9:10–17; 15:1–2; 22:14–30; 24:28–35; Acts 1:4–5; 10:41), the Jerusalem apostles (Luke 22:30; Acts 2:42, 46; 4:34–37; 6:1–6; 10:23), and Paul (Acts 11:27–30; 12:25; 20:11, 34–35; 27:33–38; 28:30–31) are all shown to be simultaneously preachers and teachers on the one hand and stewards of material goods, especially food, on the other. To these passages we could of course add those that depict Jesus and the early Christians as healers.

This unified ministry of word and table facilitates the welcoming of strangers *inside* the church as well as outside. Thus, the Hellenist and Hebrew factions of the Jerusalem church are said to have achieved reconciliation by means of an expanded *diakonia* through which the congregation's material resources were more fairly distributed (6:1–6).[36] Likewise, the delivery of money for food by the Jewish-Gentile congregation in Antioch to the famine-stricken Jerusalem church creates a new level of trust between two very different groups of believers (11:27–30; 12:25). Larrimore Crockett has called this transaction "a 'banquet' of major proportions," a symbol for Luke of

God's intention "to save both Jews and gentiles and bring them into a productive mutual relationship."[37]

Nevertheless, as many interpreters have shown, the major thrust of Luke-Acts is the outward mission of the church to the world. Above all, Luke wants his special target audience of residential believers to understand that both the quality of their life together and the ways in which they reach out to make contact with their nonbelieving neighbors will prove crucial to the continued success of this mission. Their house churches must become banquet communities where the table of the Lord (Luke 22:30) is spread for all. Residential believers in particular have a responsibility to preach the gospel through the generous disposition of their material goods. Much of the counsel regarding possessions in the Third Gospel and Acts would be understood by Luke's readers to support the welcoming of outsiders:

> Love your enemies, and do good, and lend, expecting nothing in return (Luke 6:35). And taking the five loaves and two fish [Jesus] looked up to heaven, and blessed and broke them, and gave them to the disciples to set before the crowds (9:16 in light of v. 11). But a Samaritan . . . went to [the robbed and beaten Jew] and bound up his wounds, pouring on oil and wine; then he set him on his own beast and brought him to an inn, and took care of him (10:33–34). When you give a dinner or banquet, do not invite your friends or your rich neighbors. . . . But . . . invite the poor, the maimed, the lame, and the blind (14:12–13). Behold, Lord, the half of my goods I [Zaccheus] give to the poor; and if I have defrauded any one of anything, I restore it fourfold (19:8). And they sold their possessions and goods and distributed them to all, as any had need. . . . And the Lord added to their number (Acts 2:45, 47). Now there was at Joppa a disciple named Tabitha. . . . She was full of good works and acts of charity (9:36). In all things I [Paul] have shown you that by so toiling one must help the weak, remembering the words of the Lord Jesus, how he said, "It is more blessed to give than to receive" (20:35). Now after some years I [Paul] came to bring to my nation alms and offerings (24:17).

Only with Acts 2:45 can a case be made that the aid described is restricted to believers, and there Luke's intention is obviously to show how this mutual assistance attracts nonbelievers (2:46–47). Again, we should add to these accounts the numerous stories of healing in Luke-Acts, many of which would be interpreted by residential readers as exhortations to restore the health of those outside their communities or natural circles of friends. In Acts see especially 3:1–10; 4:14–16; 8:7–8; 9:10–19; 14:8–10; 16:6–18; 19:11–20; 28:8–9.

If we should complain to Luke that his mission policies encourage the development of "rice Christians," he would probably answer that we have missed the main point, namely, that it is *God's* salvation that brings about "times of refreshing" to those in physical need (Acts 3:19). The Spirit leads; we follow. To be sure, repentance is required, and the fullness of the Spirit is expected; but these may come before, during, or after the restoration of the body. Here we have only to remember the prodigal son, whose repentance began with what is best called an opportunistic use of his imagination: "But when he came to himself, he said, 'How many of my father's hired servants have bread enough and to spare, but I perish here with hunger! I will arise and go to my father.' " (Luke 15:17–18).

But material welcomings in the Spirit are not always a matter of attracting the physically needy. Barnabas was a man of means; he did not require food, lodging, or bodily healing. Nevertheless, some deep need in him was touched by the common life of the first believers in Jerusalem, and the result was a firmer commitment (or conversion) to the young church's mission. "Thus, Joseph who was surnamed by the apostles Barnabas . . . sold a field which belonged to him, and brought the money and laid it at the apostles' feet" (4:36–37).[38] Another variation on this theme occurs in the story of an unsuccessful attempt by some Jewish exorcists in Ephesus to cast out a demon through the invoking of Jesus' name. When they themselves fall prey to the demon's power (probably because they regard Jesus' name only as a charm), many new believers, who are still practicing magical arts of various kinds, recant publicly and burn their arcane books, said to be valued at fifty thousand pieces of silver. Luke concludes this story by noting, "So the word of the Lord grew and prevailed mightily" (19:13–20). The sequence here seems to be that the new believers are shocked into giving up something of great monetary value, and this renunciation then has an evangelical consequence. Likewise in Ephesus the guild of silversmiths, whose prosperity depends upon the production and sale of little shrines devoted to the goddess Artemis, feels threatened by the effectiveness "throughout all Asia" of Paul's preaching against deities made with hands. Here it is apparent that the "considerable number of people" who have stopped buying shrines are not only Christians (19:23–27). Luke's readers need to know that their common life of preaching, healing, sharing, and so on, may well challenge the economic status quos of their pagan neighbors. Some will experience this challenge as a welcome and be led toward faith, but others will try to persecute the church.

In completing our investigation of mission as spiritual-material welcoming, we should ask whether Luke devotes any thought to the *production* of the church's material resources. There are some hints of an answer to this question. It is reasonably clear, for example, that Luke expected the church to attract a great many new members and that these, mostly Gentiles unaccustomed to generous sharing,[39] would soon learn to give substantial percentages of their goods to the community's life and mission. That Luke anticipated members with considerable wealth is suggested by his interest in the conversions of Lydia and other "leading women," who may well have played prominent roles in the financing of house churches known to him (Acts 16:14–40; 17:4, 12). Indeed, as we have seen, a good case can be made that in both Luke and Acts our author credits most of his readers with the possession of resources and urges them on toward more magnanimous sharing.[40] To readers of more average means Luke holds up the example of the humble artisan Paul, who labors so zealously at his craft that he is able to support not only himself and his associates but also "the weak" of the Ephesian community (20:34–35).

Finally, however, we must conclude that Luke simply trusts in God's abundance. Indeed, his guidance on this subject comes chiefly from sayings of Jesus, probably transmitted to him by his wandering charismatic predecessors:

> Give, and it will be given to you; good measure, pressed down, shaken together, running over, will be put into your lap. For the measure you give will be the measure you get back (6:38). Seek God's kingdom, and these [material] things shall be yours as well. Fear not, little flock, for it is your Father's good pleasure to give you the kingdom. Sell your possessions and give alms; provide yourselves with purses that do not grow old . . . (12:31–33). It is more blessed to give than to receive (Acts 20:35).

This Jesus, we learn from Luke's two-volume work, not only enacts what he says as an example to his followers but also pours out the

Holy Spirit upon them to gladden their hearts and empower them for "trading" with God's gifts (Luke 19:13–27). In the Spirit he is present to "gird himself and have them sit at table and come and serve them" (12:37).[41]

THE SUPPER OF JOYFUL REPENTANCE

And so we return once again to the centrality of the meal, for this event, more than any other, provides a locus for the paradigms and climaxes of Luke's two-volume story. Here, more clearly and consistently than anywhere else, God's purpose for humanity reveals itself in everyday history. If we were to ask Luke for a single word to describe what people do in their meal encounters with the divine, he would probably answer, "Repent!" But this single word is no simple answer. Below we shall explore some of the nuances that our author attaches to the experience of "repentance" (usually denoted by the verb *metanoein* and the noun *metanoia*).

Much of the material in Luke-Acts supports our usual understanding of the word "repentance." For example, the term describes a fundamental change of heart and mind characterized by feelings of remorse and the confession of guilt (Luke 15:17–19; 17:3–4; Acts 2:37). It includes the forsaking of destructive behavior (Luke 3:8–9; 16:3; 17:3–4) and functions as a prelude or doorway to faith (Acts 19:4; 20:21) and the forgiveness of sin (Luke 3:3; 17:3–4; 24:47; Acts 2:38; 3:19; 5:31). From repentance follow baptism (Luke 3:3; Acts 2:38; 13:24), the reception of the Holy Spirit (Acts 2:38; 19:5–10), and a new mode of life, that is, "fruits worthy of [it]" (Luke 3:8; Acts 26:20). Repentance is hardly a one-time event; it is not limited to those who are coming to faith for the first time (Luke 17:3–4). Without constant repentance everyone will perish (Luke 13:3–5). To repent means to turn from death to life (Acts 11:18), from false gods to the one true God of Israel (Acts 26:20). Repentance occurs when one receives a new knowledge of God which overpowers ignorance and penetrates the heart with its truth (Luke 3:1–18; 24:32; Acts 2:37; 3:17–19). Through this knowledge God commands (Acts 17:30) but also bestows a transformed life (Acts 5:31; 11:18). In repentance we are dealing with an act that requires human initiative but can come about only through a fresh vision or proclamation of God's goodness (Luke 15:17–18; Acts 2:22–36). At its inception, therefore, repentance is a kind of enticement, an invitation from God (Luke 14:16–24; 15:1–2), or a repossession by God, as in the parable of the lost sheep and lost coin (15:3–10).

But we have not yet touched upon what Luke considers to be the fullness of repentance. Given our author's predisposition toward deeds of justice, we would expect him to tie these closely with repentance. And he does (Luke 3:7–9; 13:1–9; 19:1–10; Acts 26:19–20). At the same time, however, he always distinguishes between repentance as such and its "fruits." Finally, the chief mark of repentance for Luke, the flower that signifies that it has really taken root, is joy. Particularly in his meal scenes Luke sets forth this distinctive view.

Thus the deep experience of joy motivates the newly converted toll collector Levi to spread a "great feast" for Jesus in his house (Luke 5:29–32). Likewise, joy emboldens the sinful woman (who has already repented and received forgiveness according to Luke 7:47) to disrupt a Pharisee's meal by washing Jesus' feet with her hair. When the shepherd finds his lost sheep and the woman recovers her lost coin, their first act is to rejoice with friends and neighbors, probably at table (Luke 15:3–10 in light of 15:1–2). Just so, Luke concludes, the angels of God rejoice in heaven over each sinner who repents (15:7, 10). Similarly, joy comes to father and younger son alike in the form of a great feast celebrating the latter's return from a wasted life in the far country (15:22–24, 32). Indeed, the elder son's only sin is that he will not take part in this lavish celebration (15:23, 32; see also 15:1–2). When Jesus invites himself to Zaccheus's house, Luke reports that the chief toll collector "made haste and came down [from the tree] and received him joyfully" (19:6). According to Luke, this exuberant hospitality then evolves into a pledge on Zaccheus's part to make restitution for his economic sins (19:8). Frederick Borsch puts it this way:

> Zaccheus's unspoken longing . . . pours out in [his] joyful reception of Jesus and burbling offer to give half his goods to the poor. . . . This is what the gospel message means by *metanoia*—a repentance that includes a changing of the mind, a new outlook on the present and the future. . . . [Zaccheus's] promises are outpourings of thanksgiving and not an effort to merit what has been given to him.[42]

On the road to Emmaus a stranger irritates two of Jesus' disciples with his challenges to their despair over their master's death. But when they nevertheless invite him to share their evening meal and he reveals himself in the breaking of bread, they experience an elation that prompts them to recall and assimilate an earlier stage of repentance: "Did not our hearts burn within us while he talked to us on the road, while he opened to us the scriptures?" (24:28–32). In his recent work *The Transforming Moment* James Loder treats this story as a paradigm for what he calls "convictional knowing," a term that closely approximates Luke's understanding of repentance. In reference to 24:30–35, Loder writes,

> As the two men "take this [broken bread] in," they are not only exposed to the brokenness they brought consciously to that room, but they are also exposed in the false hopes they brought into their relationship with Jesus in the first place. . . . Thus the *broken body* received from the *risen* Lord presents a whole new reality, a startling way of looking at things. . . . Following Jesus' disappearance, the two men experienced a coalescence within and correlatively a power of new being.[43]

In the buoyancy of this new conviction, which Luke would call "repentance into life," the two men "bear fruits which befit repentance" and return to Jerusalem that very evening to announce their good fortune at what turns out to be another meal encounter with the risen Christ (24:36–49).

When we turn to Acts, we find that here also Luke displays patterns of joyful repentance in connection with meals. Thus, the inhabitants of Jerusalem who respond positively to Peter's Pentecost sermon are said to have joined *koinōnia* groups (2:42) where "they partook of food with glad and generous hearts" (2:46). In a parallel speech, which follows upon his healing of a man born lame, Peter urges the crowd of onlookers to "Repent . . . and turn again, that your sins may be blotted out, that times of refreshing may come from the presence of the Lord" (Acts 3:19). Probably these times of refreshing are thought to be available in the banquetlike gatherings of the church. According to Acts 9:17–19, Paul's reception into the church of Damascus culminates in a meal with his new cobelievers. Although rejoicing is not explicitly mentioned, it is strongly suggested by the report that Paul has just been healed, filled with the Spirit, and baptized.

Peter, upon learning from a heavenly vision that "what God has cleansed [he] must not call common," begins to practice this insight by offering food and lodging to Cornelius's emissaries, at least one of whom is a Gentile (10:9–23). Peter's act of hospitality is the germ of his repentance from a conviction that the gospel should be preached only to Jews. When he takes the further step of visiting Cornelius's household in Caesarea and actually tells the story of Jesus to his Gentile hosts, the Holy Spirit miraculously descends upon them. This conversion brings about the completion of Peter's repentance, with the result that everyone present can rejoice in God's mercy as brothers and sisters. And now the new believer Cornelius provides food and lodging (10:44—11:3).

Paul's missionary journeys supply further examples of the joyful hospitality extended by new converts. The story of Lydia's coming to faith concludes this way: "And when she was baptized, with her household, she besought us, saying, 'If you have judged me to be faithful to the Lord, come to my house and stay.' And she prevailed upon us" (16:15). The strong words "besought" and "prevailed" imply an enthusiasm that needs to express itself in the common life of the table. On a similar note, the Philippian jailer, who has experienced conversion through Paul's preaching of the gospel, completes his baptism by providing a meal for his prisoners-become-cobelievers: "Then he brought [Paul and Silas] up into his house, and set food before them; and he rejoiced with all his household that he had believed in the Lord" (16:34). Finally, a celebration of repentance at table is probably implied when Luke describes Paul's welcoming of "all who came to him" in his Roman house-prison to learn about the kingdom of God and the Lord Jesus Christ (28:30–31).

But we have not yet examined that one meal that must be seen as the generative symbol for all other meals in Luke-Acts, namely, the supper Jesus held with his disciples on the night of his arrest. Is it also characterized by joyful repentance? The matter is not so clear. For one thing, Luke holds the view that Jesus neither ate nor drank with his disciples, despite his earnest desire to do so (22:15–23). Moreover, our author's account of the supper contains material (much of it unique to his Gospel or uniquely placed into this context) that depicts a general consternation over the announcement that Jesus' betrayer will be one of his own disciples (vv. 21–23), a quarrel over greatness among the disciples (vv. 24–30), and a prophecy by Jesus of Peter's denial (vv. 31–34). The mood of this supper can hardly be called joyful. Nor do we detect any commemoration of a recent repentance.

And yet repentance is very much in the air. Perhaps Jesus' indirect exposure of Judas is an offering of one last chance. Certainly the disciples as a whole are called upon to repent of their pride by Jesus' words on lordship and his self-designation as "one who serves" at table (vv. 25–27). Peter's repentance is foretold in the prediction of his denial (vv. 31–32). In addition, the necessity of repenting from the expectation that one will always be cared for by residents (see 17:7–10) is implied in vv. 35–36.

But there is more, for the repentance demanded and/or predicted in this last supper account is also "given" through evangelical words of Jesus. Thus, Luke alone records Jesus' expression of strong affection for his disciples as he commences his presidency over the Passover meal (vv. 15–16). Again, our author is the only evangelist to link the phrase "for you" with Jesus' bread and cup words, as if to highlight his providential care for his followers. Likewise, it is Luke's account and no other that contains a promise by Jesus that his disciples will "eat and drink at my table in my kingdom and sit on thrones judging the twelve tribes of Israel" (v. 30). Finally, Luke alone preserves Jesus' assurance to Peter that his prayer for the latter will keep his faith from failing *precisely in his denial* so that once he has repented he will be able to "strengthen [his] brethren" from a position of special leadership (v. 32).

In summary, we may say that here in his account of the last supper Luke constructs a ritual foundation for the joyful repentance that occurs at other meals in Luke-Acts. Central to Luke's last supper are words about guests and hosts (vv. 24–30). The disciples want to be lordly hosts with authority *over* their sisters and brothers. Jesus requires them to be guests in his presence so they can learn to be servant hosts. If they continue to eat at Jesus' table in his kingdom, they will in fact exercise authority, that is, the authority of Israel's ancient Spirit-filled judges to restore their nation without installing themselves as monarchs over it.[44] What we have then in vv. 24–30 is an exhortation to repent from false leadership to true leadership. It takes place at the meal of meals and requires table imagery for its proper understanding. We must suspect that Luke wants to encourage the repetition of this host-guest-host cycle of repentance at future celebrations of the Lord's Supper in his own day. It is a liturgy for the continuing transformation of power in the church. Luke tells other stories about the varieties of joyful repentance that can be expected to take place at meals of the church (e.g., Luke 24:28–35; Acts 2:42–47), but his account of the last supper grounds them.

CONCLUSIONS

We began our investigation of hospitality in Luke-Acts by taking note of Minear's rather sweeping assertion that for Luke "table fellowship as interpreted by table talk constituted the gospel." We attempted to test Minear's view by examining the interrelationships between travelers and residents that Luke is advocating. This process led us to the conclusion that our author writes primarily to residents, though without denigrating the impressive achievements of the wandering charismatic missionaries (which continue, to some degree, in his day). Indeed, the goal for Luke on this issue is a cooperative missionary effort characterized by a fluidity in guest and host roles on the part of travelers and residents alike. From these role reversals, which take place most often in house churches and typically at meals, diverse spiritual-material welcomings are generated. As a consequence, local churches must function as *(a)* banquet communities which attract their nonbelieving neighbors and *(b)* home bases for missionaries who travel but tend to settle down in younger churches for extended residencies as teacher-colleagues and leaders-by-example. This missionary enterprise brings with it a growing network of mutual concern among the churches which includes the material aid and instruction in the gospel offered by the younger churches to their sisters and brothers in Jerusalem.[45]

Throughout Luke's two-volume story progress in partnership is sustained by the intervention of God and Jesus, chiefly through the agency of the Holy Spirit. Humans come to know God's saving plan more deeply *(epignōskein)* and participate in it more fully through acts of repentance. In many cases these coincide with the role reversals mentioned above. In every case their characteristic mark is joy, and this is frequently expressed in meal celebrations. To conclude, then, we may say that when we allow the word "gospel" to embrace both repentance and mission, and when we place "table fellowship/table talk" within the broader category of hospitality,

120   *NEW TESTAMENT HOSPITALITY*

Minear's aphorism proves strikingly accurate. Through the interaction of guests and hosts, changing their roles as the Spirit leads them, the word of the Lord grows. It is a lesson worth learning—and relearning.

NOTES

1. From among recent works on Luke-Acts, our summary draws especially upon those by Paul Minear, "Dear Theo: The Kerygmatic Intention and Claim of the Book of Acts," *Interpretation* 27 (1973): 131–50; Robert Karris, "Missionary Communities: A New Paradigm for the Study of Luke-Acts," *CBQ* 41 (1979): 80–97; Richard Dillon, *From Eye-Witnesses to Ministers of the Word* (Rome: Biblical Institute Press, 1978), and "Previewing Luke's Project from His Prologue (Luke 1:1–4)," *CBQ* 43 (1981): 205–27.
2. I have stressed this in my *Jews and Christians in Dialogue*.
3. It is treated this way by H. J. Cadbury in "Lexical Notes on Luke-Acts: Luke's Interest in Lodging," *JBL* 45 (1926): 305–22, and *The Making of Luke-Acts* (London: SPCK, 1968), 249–53; D. Riddle, "Early Christian Hospitality: A Factor in the Gospel Transmission," *JBL* 57 (1938): 151–53; Malherbe, *Social Aspects of Early Christianity*, 66–67; Donald Juel, *Luke-Acts: the Promise of History* (Atlanta: John Knox Press, 1983), 88–90.
4. Paul Minear, *Commands of Christ: Authority and Implications* (Nashville: Abingdon Press, 1972), 180.
5. H. Evans, "Barnabas the Bridge-Builder," *ET* 89 (1977): 248–50; Brown and Meier, *Antioch and Rome*, 33–35.
6. J. Navone, "The Lukan Banquet Community," *Bible Today* 51 (1970): 155–61.
7. Frederick Buechner, *Love Feast* (San Francisco: Harper & Row, 1984), 56.
8. Cadbury, *Making of Luke-Acts*, 249–50.
9. C. F. Evans, "The Central Section in St. Luke's Gospel," in *Studies in the Gospels*, ed. D. E. Nineham (Oxford: Basil Blackwell & Mott, 1955), 50. This quotation, as well as much of the SL material just cited, came to me through Paul Minear's *To Heal and to Reveal: The Prophetic Vocation according to Luke* (New York: Seabury Press, 1976), 111 and passim.
10. Dillon, *From Eye-Witnesses to Ministers of the Word*, 240–46; 252–60.
11. Ibid., 264–65.
12. See Theissen's *Sociology of Early Palestinian Christianity*.
13. Dillon, *From Eye-Witnesses to Ministers of the Word*, 239.
14. Ibid., 242.
15. They can be discerned, e.g., in 2 Corinthians 10—13 and Matt. 19:11–12, as well as in *Didache* 11–12. The elder who wrote 2 and 3 John may have been a kind of wandering missionary. See esp. 2 John 10—11; 3 John 5—10.

Finally, the second-century bishop of Hieropolis, Papias, seems to have considered some of the visitors he received itinerant heirs of the apostles. In his view they taught him far more about the gospel through their oral chain of tradition than he could glean from written documents. See Eusebius, *Ecclesiastical History*, III.39.1–7.

16. Theissen, "Itinerant Radicalism: The Tradition of Jesus Sayings from the Perspective of Sociology of Literature," 91.

17. Minear, *To Heal and to Reveal*, 87. Joseph Barnabas, considered by Luke to be exemplary for his readers (see esp. 11:24), is said to have received his second name from the apostles. According to Luke, it means "son of encouragement" (*huios paraklēseōs; Acts* 4:36). But in both Hebrew and Aramaic "Barnabas" means something closer to "son of a prophet." These two meanings are not incompatible because Luke, like Paul, thinks of prophecy within a congregation chiefly in terms of *paraklēsis* (Acts 2:40; 11:23; 14:22; 15:31–32; 20:1–2; 21:10–12; 27:33–34). See E. Earle Ellis, "The Role of the Christian Prophet in Acts," in *Apostolic History and the Gospel: Biblical Essays Presented to F. F. Bruce on His 60th Birthday*, ed. Ward Gasque and Ralph Martin (Grand Rapids: Wm. B. Eerdmans, 1970).

18. See, among others, Dillon, *From Eye-Witnesses to Ministers of the Word*, 269.

19. Theissen comes close to this position in "Itinerant Radicalism," 91.

20. Robin Scroggs calls attention to a distinction made by Gradon Snyder between "trans-local tradition" and "local tradition" in early Christian history. These two strains exist in tension and must usually reach some compromise if the institution they represent is to flourish. See Scroggs, "The Sociological Interpretation of the New Testament," *NTS* 26 (1980): 172. If we apply this typology to Acts, it is easy to see Luke in the role of chief mediator.

21. Robert Karris, "Poor and Rich: The Lukan Sitz im Leben," in *Perspectives in Luke-Acts*, ed. C. H. Talbert (Danville, Va.: Association of Baptist Professors of Religion, 1978), 112–25. See also Walter Pilgrim, *Good News to the Poor: Wealth and Poverty in Luke-Acts* (Minneapolis: Augsburg Pub. House, 1981), esp. 160–75. In his *Sharing Possessions: Mandate and Symbol of Faith*, 23, Johnson expresses doubt that Luke's inconsistent talk about possessions can be made to fit into any schemes based on periods of time or a specialized readership. My own research, however, tends to confirm the conclusions of Karris and Pilgrim.

22. In Matt. 19:22 and Mark 10:22 it is clear that the man has made a definite decision not to sell his possessions and follow Jesus.

23. Evidence presented below in "Mission as Spiritual-Material Welcoming" makes it probable that the "manifold more" of 18:30 is not confined to spiritual goods.

24. In Matthew's version of this saying (24:45) the word for food *(trophē)* is quite general and could denote any kind of material or spiritual nourishment. But Luke's *sitometrion* means quite literally "a measure of grain."

25. Paul Minear, "A Note on Luke 17:7–10," *JBL* 93 (1974): 85.

26. Ibid., 86.

27. Thus Minear's conclusion in *To Heal and to Reveal*, 83, that Luke "viewed the church as a group of charismatic communities linked together by itinerant charismatic leaders" does not give sufficient weight to our author's support for *residential charismatic leaders*.

28. Luke conceives of the house as a large one with some kind of public courtyard (1:15; 2:1, 5–14).

29. Pilgrim, *Good News to the Poor*, 151.

30. Precisely as "evangelist" Philip lives in a house.

31. Mortimer Arias, "Centripetal Mission or Evangelization by Hospitality," *Missiology: An International Review* 10 (1982): 69–81.

32. Whether or not a final break between church and synagogue has taken place by Luke's time, he seems to be telling his readers that the use of Jewish institutions for missionary purposes is now passé.

33. Our conclusions in this section both derive from and support a number of the views expressed by Karris in his "Missionary Communities." See n. 1 above.

34. Marshall Frady, *Southerners: A Journalist's Odyssey* (New York: New American Library, 1980), 382.

35. In Acts we may think of Paul's own call/conversion (9:1–19, etc.), as well as the commissioning of Paul and Barnabas (13:1–4) and the choosing of Mark, Silas, and Timothy to be itinerant coworkers (15:36—16:4). Luke surely expects such changes of status to occur in the church of his day. Furthermore, it seems to me that because Luke typically holds up heroes and heroines of faith as examples, he would have expected the calls to discipleship narrated in his Gospel to summon a number of his residential readers to the itinerant life.

36. Although 6:1–6 is often cited as evidence for the sanctioning of a division in the word and table ministries of Luke's day, there is no real basis for this view in the text. The Twelve are not said to give up their table ministry. Rather, they wish to place limits on it so as not to shortchange their ministry of the word. In 6:4 "devote ourselves" *(proskarterein)* does not mean to choose one thing to the exclusion of another but simply to "be faithful to" the former or be "busily engaged in" it. With the interpretation proposed here there is no mystery about the fact that the seven Hellenists appointed to diaconal work are *also* powerful preachers and miracle workers (6:8—8:13).

37. Larrimore Crockett, "Luke 4:25–27 and Jewish-Gentile Relations in Luke-Acts," *JBL* 88 (1969): 181.

38. The story is narrated as if many believers had already redistributed their wealth before Barnabas came on the scene (4:32–35). Presumably, he then perceived the "great grace [which] was upon them all" (4:33; note the par. with 11:23) and was moved to offer up the proceeds from his land.

39. Pilgrim, *Good News to the Poor*, 150.

40. See n. 21 above.

41. Although this passage refers in the strict sense to the Parousia, Luke's stories of the last supper and of the Risen One's self-disclosure to two disciples on the road to Emmaus strongly imply that he wants his readers to anticipate Christ's *diakonia* to them in their eucharists (see also Acts 1:4).

42. Frederick H. Borsch, *Power in Weakness: New Hearing for Gospel Stories of Healing and Discipleship* (Philadelphia: Fortress Press, 1983), 29.

43. James Loder, *The Transforming Moment: Understanding Convictional Experiences* (San Francisco: Harper & Row, 1981), 103, 107.

44. For Luke, this begins to happen in the everyday life of the Jerusalem church. See Jacob Jervell, *Luke and the People of God: A New Look at Luke-Acts* (Minneapolis: Augsburg Pub. House, 1972), 75–112.

45. At the same time Paul, who certainly represents the younger churches as far as Luke is concerned, accepts instruction from believers in Jerusalem so that the mother congregration's credibility with its neighbors will not be placed in jeopardy (Acts 21:17–26).

CHAPTER 5

Frontiers
of Hospitality

Our chapter title can be understood in at least three ways. The word "frontier" may refer first of all to the outer edge of a civilized area or a discrete field of knowledge; and so in this last chapter it will denote the transposition of our exegetical results into summary statements about the contours and textures of what we have been calling New Testament hospitality. A second meaning for "frontier," more common in Europe perhaps, has to do with the border or marginal area of land that separates two countries. Anyone who crosses such boundaries with regularity will know how well defined they seem—complete with armed guards, gates, electronic surveillance, and so on—but how, on closer inspection, they prove to be mysteriously vague and therefore subject to dispute. This sense of the word "frontier" fits well with our topic, for we have learned that New Testament hospitality centers upon meetings and transactions with strangers that are characterized by the shifting of guest and host roles, and even (it is claimed) by acts of God. Here we may think of what Victor Turner and others have termed "liminal" experiences, of thresholds and half-opened doors into holy spaces. Finally, we can sometimes discern in the word "frontier" a quality of motion, as if the boundary itself were rushing forward even as we stand upon it or, alternatively, coming at us from some unknown place. As examples, we may cite the "new frontiers" proclaimed by John F. Kennedy or the vast reaches of human consciousness and outer space which call out to us for exploration. In terms of our study, language about the kingdom of God is analogous to this kind of mobile frontier. The kingdom breaks in on meals and other occasions of welcoming; or it somehow advances through alliances with strangers. Indeed, we have discovered that in the eyes of Jesus, Paul, and Luke the kingdom often turns out to be both cause and consequence of hospitality. The three facets of the term "frontier" just noted will not be treated separately. Nor shall we always be able to distinguish one from the other within our chapter subdivisions. Nevertheless, all three will be present, most of the time, as the dynamic that shapes our thoughts.

One last word about the shape of this chapter needs to be added here. I have elected to make of it not so much a systematic presentation of results as an essay on horizons, that is, an attempt to show how the data from our exegetical chapters lead us in certain directions, sensitize us to particular issues of hospitality in our own day, and help to equip us for ministries that respond effectively to them. In other words, this final chapter presumes to be a kind of overture to biblical theology at the practical level. It is at most an overture, not an opera.

PARTNERSHIP WITH STRANGERS TODAY

Unless we live in isolated rural areas, encounters with strangers are likely to form a normal part of our everyday routine. But few of these contacts ever become partnerships in the New Testament sense, where members learn to know one another as coparticipants in the power of the kingdom and companion-builders of God's home on earth, where hospitality becomes the generative foundation for ethics. It would be a romantic illusion to suppose that we could form such partnerships with all the strangers we meet, including those intimate strangers who make up our household and circles of friends. Nevertheless, in moments of clarity we are likely to sense that precisely in our contacts with strangers far more doors to the feast of the kingdom open up than we are willing to enter. How can we move toward greater maturity in our vocation as the guests and hosts of God?

Above all, we need to grow in our ability simply to identify potential and actual practices of New Testament hospitality. This, however, requires moving through the ordinary events of our days with a readiness for partnership. We shall have more to say about the cultivation of such a readiness below, but we may begin to define it here. Perhaps it is best described as a space inside us—part of what

Henry Nouwen calls "free space"[1]—which welcomes marginal people because it expects them to be bearers of God's abundance or catalysts for it. Jesus ate with outcasts; Paul and Luke took strong stands on behalf of those relegated to the position of second-class citizens in the church. They did so, our research has shown, because they knew that God *by nature* recruits outsiders to be partners in providence, makes a home among them, and through them enriches the world. We miss out on this fullness of life when we limit our partnerships to those who most resemble ourselves.

The inner space with which we are concerned is no empty room, waiting passively to be filled by whoever happens to drop in. Instead, it may be likened to a laboratory in which new modes of welcoming and being welcomed are created, in which our imaginations play upon the innumerable combinations of guest and host roles, while scanning the world outside for opportunities to enact them. This is not a frantic activity but one that grows quietly out of faith in Jesus Christ as our access to God's banquet hall (Rom. 5:2). Even at its best, however, our inner space cannot itself provide a home for the external stranger. God will grant that to the stranger, while calling upon us to help in building up the spiritual and material environments that make it possible.

Any meeting of strangers is a potential time and place for partnership, but meetings with festive atmospheres are prime candidates. This is so because at such events strangers gather, for the most part, without rigid agendas. At parties we are more likely than at other times to experiment with new social relationships, to take on roles we would otherwise reject as foolish or improper. The classic institutionalization of such festivities in nineteenth- and twentieth-century Christianity known to most North Americans is the church supper. It is said that in some Harlem churches the meal functions as a natural continuation of the Sunday service, an agapē feast that serves to incarnate the preaching, singing, and praying. At the Mother African Methodist Episcopal Zion Church, the oldest organized black congregation in New York City, this tradition dates back at least to the Civil War period when men and women who had escaped slavery in the South emerged from the Underground Railroad to be welcomed as free citizens.[2]

Not many of our church meals can claim such a noble heritage, but most of them have all the raw materials needed for creating partnership with strangers. The special vocation of those sensitive to the precepts of New Testament hospitality, here as in secular celebrations, is to search for openings that help people move beyond the conventions of this age and into the abundance of God's banquet hall. At such thresholds we must be prepared to hear and to speak prophetically.[3] By keeping the language of secular and church business to a minimum, we shall find that simple liturgies and old hymns take on powerful meanings. People who do not know one another or who know but dislike one another may well be moved by the conjunction of table sharing and holy words to seek new relationships with their neighbors.

Here we cannot fail to mention that central meal of the church called Eucharist, for in this many-leveled feast the exchanges we are describing find ritual expression. Readers may recall that each of our exegetical chapters contains a short essay on the eucharistic meal constructed, respectively, from the viewpoint of Jesus, Paul, and Luke. We found that the supper was variously interpreted as a preparation for hosts of the kingdom, as a time of special discernment during which all participants were to see themselves engaged in a holy communion of gift sharing with their sisters and brothers, and finally, as an occasion for joyful repentance, especially a turning from false to true leadership. Unfortunately few of our eucharistic celebrations today allow space for these activities to happen in a corporate way or come to verbal expression for the benefit of the whole congregation. I suppose I am once again advocating prophecy in the New Testament sense, or something like the testimonies of the gospel churches. At any rate, I suspect that those of us in the so-called liturgical churches can make better use of the time currently allotted to "passing the peace." Or we might combine the sacrament more often than we do with a real supper, as Paul apparently envisioned it. Naturally changes like this require a good deal of preparation and a structure that encourages small group interaction. As far as I can tell, all reflections on eucharistic hospitality in the New Testament presuppose a house church setting.

Of absolute importance for New Testament hospitality, wherever it occurs, is the ministry of introduction. I name Barnabas as its patron saint, for he was the one person who dared to build a bridge of understanding between the recently converted Paul and the suspicious believers of Jerusalem who doubted if their persecutor had really seen the light (Acts 9:26–27). In the risky business of bringing alienated people together, introducers must see through the stereotypes and fears that prevent mutual welcoming so as to claim ground for the powerful exchange of gifts which happens when partnerships between strangers are actually forged. Wilfred Bockelman is engaged in such a ministry. I know him only through his newsletter, *The Eye of the Needle: A Monthly Perspective for the Responsible Use of Wealth, Power and Position*,[4] but I applaud his efforts to persuade us that individuals or groups who shrink from giving one another so much as a first hearing may prove eventually to be allies on important issues. For example, Bockelman is fond of showing us liberal Christians how representatives of large corporations, whom we often dismiss as servants of greed, sometimes bring insights into the gospel that have not been revealed to us.

Parker Palmer affirms the ministry of introduction when he states that one of the church's major vocations in the public sphere is

> to host dialogues between groups in the community who are, or may be, in conflict . . . [i.e.], such groups as teachers and school boards, teenagers and police, blacks and whites in "changing neighborhoods," labor and management, "gays" and "straights."[5]

Palmer might have added: "advocates of a nuclear freeze and proponents of a strong national defense." Usually we gain more than we give in facilitating such partnerships. An important proviso in working out agendas is that churches must try to provide as much hospitable space for their own members as they do for strangers.[6] But of course we also need to remember that hospitable space for Christians always comes with the built-in challenge to become hosts!

In my own experience ministries of introduction and other practices of hospitality often find their impetus within structures of contradiction. By these I mean systems or institutions in our society that promise hospitality but do not or cannot deliver it. Here my work as a hospital chaplain comes to mind. Our primary institution for healing, which by its very name claims to be a haven for those in physical or mental distress, all too frequently instills fear and alienation among its guests. This is not the place to address such problems in detail or to assign blame. Indeed, no one who works in a hospital for long can fail to notice the staggering number of double-bind situations that confront medical and administrative staff workers. The point here is simply to note that hospitable spaces for troubled sufferers can often occur when people on the margin, who are not quite owned by institutional categories, insert themselves into official procedures and become agents of God's kingdom. Obviously chaplains and other practitioners of religion are not the only people who do this work, but they, more than others, must take responsibility for keeping it alive.

To hospitals we may add several other structures of contradiction. Henri Nouwen has given us poignant sketches of the mutual welcoming between parents and children or teachers and students that is crippled or aborted by human pride.[7] In this context most of us can recall forms of hospitality, given or received, which were actually nothing more than occasions for competition and domination. Indeed, we remember that Jesus fought such problems within his own group of disciples, probably to the day of his death. And yet the uniform expectation of Jesus, Paul, and Luke was that even in these mockeries of hospitality God's love would open up doors for compassionate sharing.

Within the Christian church today there are communities that take this hope seriously and thus set a high priority upon establishing partnerships with strangers. I have in mind particularly "intentional" communities like the Church of the Saviour or Sojourners in Washington, D.C., which devote themselves to marginal people and unpopular causes. I do not mean to idealize such groups or propose them as substitutes for the typical parish churches of our denominations. Sometimes intentional groups practice their own brands of exclusivism. By and large, however, they treasure diversity; they expect the stranger to be a bearer and evoker of gifts among them. Elizabeth O'Conner's description of the Ram's Horn Feast held at the Church of the Saviour dovetails with what we have learned about Pauline and Lukan table sharing:

> The community which gathers for the feast is made up of . . . the old, the maimed, the halt, the educated and not so educated. Some are successful, some are so-called "dropouts." A few like to speak in intellectual terms, and a few like to speak in tongues. We are from churches housed in storefronts and from churches with impressive towers. In all, we make

> a strange company, but that is the way we want it to be. We meet to celebrate our common humanity and to read and ponder Scripture and to wait for the empowering of the Spirit.[8]

As for the Sojourners, what impresses me most is their commitment to building productive relationships with Christians from abroad, especially those from Third World countries.

But talk of partnerships with the Third World must prompt a venture into the material dimensions of hospitality. We remember that Jesus, Paul, and Luke all thought of welcoming in terms of sharing goods and services at the threshold of God's kingdom. Real economic transactions were envisioned. Indeed, it is worth noting that the word "economics" derives from the Greek *oikonomia*, which literally means "management of a household." Within the framework of New Testament hospitality, with its stress on community life, we do well to posit and explore an economics of the Spirit.

THE ECONOMICS OF THE SPIRIT

There is a fearful poverty at large in the world today, much of it just around the corner from us, a good deal of it among Christians. And there are inequities of status that crush the human spirit even in the midst of material wealth. Fragile systems of survival, based on the interdependence of rich and poor or high and low, have become a fact of modern life. Tremendous problems pulse within these not so blessed ties that bind. New Testament hospitality itself cannot present comprehensive solutions to the world's socioeconomic woes, but it may call us back to the conviction that God is always creating spaces for mutuality where we see only enmity and selfishness. New Testament hospitality, like its Jewish parent, has an inherent passion for the redemption of the material order. And so we must investigate the economics of the Spirit.

The thesis I want to propose as an exposition of this phrase grows out of our exegetical work. It is that God has built a secret abundance into the scheme of things, an abundance that can more than fill our needs when we seek to form partnerships for the kingdom. This thesis has a corollary, namely, that hospitality, as understood in the New Testament writings, presumes a reciprocity between God's abundance and human acts of sacrifice. Both prove fundamental for the establishment of community life with those who are different from (and therefore "unequal" to) ourselves. Our basic task then is to take a closer look at this dialectic of sacrifice and abundance so as to familiarize ourselves with its inner workings. It is probably best to state at the outset that I take "sacrifice" in its original sense of making something sacred by offering it up to God. Sacrifice does not refer first of all to loss or deprivation, although feelings of loss and deprivation may well accompany sacrificial acts.

Jesus, Paul, and Luke had much to say about the interplay between sacrifice and abundance. We shall profit from reviewing just a few of their pronouncements:

> Abba, hallowed be thy name,
> Thy kingdom come,
> Our bread for tomorrow give us today,
> And forgive us our debts as we also herewith
>   forgive our debtors
>   (Luke 11:2-4)[9]

> In a severe test of affliction [the Macedonians'] abundance of joy and their extreme poverty have overflowed in a wealth of liberality on their part. For they gave [money for the Jerusalem relief fund] according to their means, as I can testify, and beyond their means of their own free will . . . , but first they gave themselves to the Lord and to us by the will of God. (2 Cor. 8:2-5)

> And God is able to provide you [Corinthians] with every blessing in abundance, so that you may always have enough of everything and may provide in abundance for every good work. (2 Cor. 9:8)

> And [the first members of the Jerusalem church] sold their possessions and goods and distributed them to all, as any had need. And day by day, attending the temple together and breaking bread in their homes, they partook of food with glad and generous hearts, praising God and having favor with all the people. And the Lord added to their number daily those who were being saved. (Acts 2:45-47)

These passages refer to quite different situations, but they have several features in common. First, in each of them it is presupposed that abundance and sacrifice intermingle so as to stimulate each other. The feast of the kingdom coming is enjoyed and anticipated; but at the same time acts of self-offering occur in the form of forgiveness or generous sharing. From our limited human perspective it is impossible to be very clear about cause-effect relationships in this matrix of giving and receiving. Second, in each passage above, a type of partnership with strangers is envisioned, a move toward reconciliation or spiritual and material reciprocity with those who are not part of one's natural circle of companions. Third, each passage stems from a conviction that God is present as the real author of both sacrifice and abundance. God's will calls them forth; God's activity empowers them. So the divine energy flows through all parties in every redemptive alliance, a fact that one can only acknowledge in the language of worship ("Abba" . . . "gave themselves to the Lord" . . . "praising God"). Letty Russell properly characterizes this whole enterprise as a partnership with God in the ongoing work of New Creation (2 Cor. 5:16—6:2). As such, it is charged with "gifts of synergy, serendipity, and sharing."[10]

But there is one more feature of the passages cited above that requires comment. In all of them the exchanges described, whether spiritual or material, grow out of social structures where membership is the primary good. Individuals are valued and welcomed as sharers together with their neighbors in the feast of the kingdom. Fundamental to the building of partnerships with strangers is a community that experiences itself as the guests of God. In sorting through this aspect of New Testament hospitality, I have found the work of the social philosopher Michael Walzer to be a useful guide. In his book *Spheres of Justice: A Defense of Pluralism and Equality*, Walzer argues that for societies generally and for all the subgroups that comprise them, membership stands prior to all other rights and therefore determines the type of distributive justice that will be practiced in each community. Because we all belong to a number of small societies, each defining the goods of membership in a particular way, we are bound to encounter conflicts when we try to achieve a just society for all. Our various "spheres" interpenetrate or collide; there is no easy harmony among them. An unusually harsh dissonance occurs when money attempts to dominate spheres where, traditionally, other values have reigned, for example, well being, honor, or divine grace. And this, Walzer asserts, is now happening in the United States on an unprecedented scale.[11] Still, he believes, democratic nations like our own continue to offer the best opportunity for diverse orbs of justice to meet and compromise so that all citizens will be able to share in a "complex equality." But this enterprise requires widespread participation in the political structures, not to mention the traditional price placed upon liberty: eternal vigilance.[12]

In effect, Walzer has provided a secular rationale for partnership with strangers. Not surprisingly, he devotes considerable attention to problems of hospitality. As a difficult case in point he cites the lot of the so-called guest-workers, mostly from Turkey and the Balkans, who contract for jobs with the governments of Switzerland, Sweden, and West Germany. These people stand to earn relatively high wages by the standards of their home countries, but in terms of political rights they are

> excluded from the company of men and women that includes other people [i.e., citizens] exactly like themselves. They are locked into an inferior position that is also an anomalous position; they are outcasts in a society that has no caste norms.[13]

Here, Walzer suggests, we have a partnership with strangers that is simply too unequal, for it withholds from these "guests" the possibility of anything close to membership in the local society. Here even complex equality is violated, for the human spirit is demeaned. From the viewpoint of justice the only solution would be one that moved toward "the protection of citizenship or potential citizenship."[14] Such a move would serve to benefit everyone over the long haul.

In arguing this way, Walzer comes close to the church's agenda for hospitality as we have seen it emerging from our exegetical work. Jesus and the first communities of believers present us with a strong bias toward inclusiveness. Their controlling vision is that everyone must have a chance to share in the feast of the kingdom and be welcomed into the new humanity. The mission that God offers the church has to do with membership in its fullest dimensions. This means that an expanding partnership with strangers proves absolutely central to the gospel and, moreover, that our alliances must tend toward socioeconomic equality. Both Walzer and the apostle Paul remind us that such an equality will be complex (see 2 Cor. 8:13–15). According to Paul, it is God's grace that works among us to bring about a fair distribution of spiritual and material goods on all sides.

New Testament hospitality must always concern itself with the nuts and bolts of justice. These will come into play first of all among the strangers best known to the church, namely, its own members; but then our frontiers will move very swiftly to the neighbors who are geographically closest to us and to those who become our special allies (or enemies) in matters involving the gospel. Here I refer especially to people who constitute blocks of power in business, government, and other religions. I think it follows from Walzer's study that subgroups in a given society, like the church, will speak most effectively to issues of justice for humankind in general when they are able to show publicly that they are doing their "homework" on the practical problems that arise from their particular traditions about membership.

In our oldest Christian sources we see a fundamental commitment to the destruction or transformation of barriers that prevent mutual love among humans. This is a socioeconomic activity, and in the New Testament it is assigned preeminently to the Holy Spirit. The Spirit blows where it wills, and hardly ever in the safe places where we want to settle down. It is the agent of fluidity that permeates or circumnavigates the barricades of impossibility we erect. The Spirit speaks within us, assuring us of our own welcome by God (Rom. 8:15–17); but it also calls us forward, leading us into new frontiers of hospitality. According to Luke especially, it is the Spirit who enables us to change our guest and host roles in ways that are appropriate to the church's mission. For both Luke and Paul, the Spirit helps us taste God's abundance even when we feel poor by the standards of this age, or when we are called upon to offer ourselves and our goods to God's purpose.

This often means challenging habitual practices of consumption in the name of a higher wealth. Elizabeth O'Conner writes:

> I do not want to be robbed of the revolutionary vocation that I have as a Christian, and I am quite confident that this is what greed does to us. In the end it leaves everyone poor. I give more attention these days to what the saints say about "self-denial," as well as more attention to what modern psychology says about the "realization of potential." These two concepts are better fellow workers than we thought.[15]

The Spirit moves to create "grace-grace" situations, that is, communions or *koinōnias* in which all parties "deny" themselves but also receive, and *expect* to receive, "good measure, pressed down, shaken together, running over" (Luke 6:38). Grace abounds because God multiplies both the giving and receiving (2 Cor. 9:8–11). From the perspective of New Testament hospitality the Spirit calls less for a "solidarity with victims"[16] than for a commitment to work alongside those who suffer grave injury or injustice in the expectation that all of us will bring gifts to one another (Rom. 1:11–12).

The Spirit is a friend of profit-sharing plans, as long as the profits are broadly defined in terms of their benefits for humanity, and as long as the sharing helps to create more equitable relationships among people of diverse socioeconomic backgrounds. There are definite implications here for the shaping of industrial policies. Some of these have been articulated by a group within the Episcopal Church called the Urban Bishops' Coalition. Though not explicitly grounded in biblical language, a recent appeal from this group, published in the *New York Times*, clearly advocates an economics of the Spirit. A portion of the bishops' message follows:

> In light of rapidly growing patterns of industrial disinvestment we ask whether it is not time to explore alternatives to corporate and conglomerate ownership that removes decision-making and control from local communities. . . . We suggest that a range of ideas, including national industrial policies that preserve communities' economic viability, and models of cooperative ownership, can help restore work to its proper role of serving the wider community. Where cooperatively owned enterprises have existed in this country and elsewhere, productivity has been high. . . . We do not see ways to achieve long-range economic recovery for people in America and elsewhere except through democratic control of work in local communities.[17]

In November 1984, the Roman Catholic bishops of the United States published the first draft of a comprehensive pastoral letter on the relationship between the church's social teaching and the American economy. It is clear from this document that the bishops think sweeping changes in our present economic structures will be required to bring about minimal justice for all citizens.[18] Although some Christians will continue to object that the church cannot speak with any authority in the socioeconomic realm, our research has indicated otherwise. The Spirit probes and redefines all frontiers of sharing, whether religious or secular; and we are called to follow its lead. In the Spirit we are all *oikonomoi* (Luke 12:42; 1 Pet. 4:10), that is, householders and stewards—or, to use the modern term which is nothing other than the English spelling of this ancient Greek word—

"economists." It is part of our core identity as Christians to become agents for the fair exchange of goods and services.

Here some last reflections on sacrifice and abundance are in order. To encourage more equitable transactions in status and wealth today, those of us blessed with special privilege—which means the writer and most readers of this book—will have to sacrifice. That may involve pain; certainly it will require discipline and effort. The cross is central to every Christian understanding of abundance (Mark 8:34–37; 14:22–25; 1 Cor. 1:18–31). But from the economics of the Spirit two principles emerge to help us. First, sacrifice begins and ends in worship as an act of sanctifying what we have by offering it up (the preposition is significant) to God. Thus we "invest" our goods for a higher purpose and profit than we are able to define through conventional analysis, whether capitalist or Marxist. That is, we declare ourselves ready to participate in God's gracious surprises, to join in socioeconomic ventures with those who are not our natural companions. Second, our sacrifice need not proceed from guilt or an economy of scarcity. Threats from desperate people who are ready to take what we have by force may indeed prompt deeds of divestment; but from the viewpoint of New Testament hospitality they are not the typical motivation for our actions. What can truly empower our sharing over the long haul is the richness in personhood and community which we already have (2 Cor. 8:9) but which even the most mature among us have only begun to appropriate. The secrets of God's abundance invite us to discover them and to live accordingly.

Often the most pressing invitations will be mediated by strangers, for the Spirit is constantly presenting us with "angels" (Acts 10:17–20; Heb. 13:2). But we must also do our part in welcoming them and joining forces with them. Essential to this process is the task of discernment, for we need to recognize where and how we can form a partnership with strangers that will bear fruit. From Paul's discussion of the Lord's Supper we recall that discernment is a spiritual activity, a quality of worship. But it often takes place in the secular world as we try to decide which individuals and groups are most attentive to God's purposes. In this next section I offer some of my own experiences with forms of ministry that seem to embody the characteristics of hospitality detailed in our exegetical chapters. My readers will have to judge whether or not my choices show discernment. My claim is only that New Testament hospitality today would have to look *something like* what follows.

DISCERNING THE FRONTIERS

My introduction to the Christian Community Service Agency of Miami came from a bumper sticker on a car parked close to its office. The message, adorned with a small cross and the letters CCSA, was simple enough. "Everyone Counts!" it said. Later, when I met and interviewed some of the people who worked for this agency, I learned that they meant it. CCSA is a Protestant group devoted to finding and helping residents of Miami who are not popular with the power structures in this busy sunbelt metropolis, or for that matter in the U.S. generally. These residents include recent immigrants from Cuba, especially the great influx of "Marielistas" who were released from prisons and hospitals; the local black community, which has often suffered eclipse in the socioeconomic developments of the past two decades; and above all, a large number of Haitian refugees, most of whom are detained in camps by immigration officials until private sponsors can demonstrate that they are capable of supporting themselves on the "outside." But even then the official government policy is to consider them illegal aliens and deport them as often as possible. The fear of AIDS certainly plays a role here.

"Everyone counts!" It is a way of saying "welcome" to the marginal people. It is a declaration of faith in the gifts brought to society by those who are often dismissed as burdens on society. One theme that kept emerging from my conversations with workers at the agency was that they were simply not willing to rest with definitions of socioeconomic problems worked out by the experts. At CCSA people saw with different eyes (or hearts); they both believed and disbelieved official government pronouncements and were consequently on the lookout for unusual partnerships. On occasion, I learned, this search produces a surprising amount of support and money from national as well as local sources in government for carrying out activities that the governments themselves declare to be impossible. Sometimes humanitarian appeals are made to individuals in high places; sometimes factual data is presented to show that official policies are not in the public interest and that until they can be changed, private agencies like CCSA offer the best hope of redressing grievances.

One of the groups affiliated with CCSA is the Belle Glade Community Service Center sponsored by the Lutheran Ministries of Florida. Belle Glade is a farming community some seventy air-miles northwest of Miami in which many Haitians have been relocated. The ministry there attempts to address broader issues of language isolation and self-confidence as well as the daily problems of poverty and ill health. Serving as pastoral leader of the center is Bernard Lacombe, a Pentecostal minister from Haiti "discovered," as he likes to put it, during a chance conversation with a Lutheran traveler at the Ft. Lauderdale airport, where he was working as a chief security officer. Directing the social work of the center is Marie St. Cyr, a Haitian who emigrated to the U.S. several years ago and completed her education in Philadelphia. There, in the midst of a promising career as psychotherapist and in conversation with Christian friends, she felt a call to join her people at the extremities of their need by moving to Florida. The first meeting between Marie and Bernard in Belle Glade turned out to be a reunion. Although he did not recognize her, Marie recalled that as a girl she had belonged to his Pentecostal congregation in Port au Prince. I have learned that one should expect such coincidences on the frontiers of hospitality.

In fact, one of them occurred during my visit to Belle Glade in 1983. At the urging of a friend, I telephoned the local Episcopal priest, Charles Farrar, and found that many years before he had studied at the General Seminary where I teach. My call was his first personal contact with his alma mater in a long time, so the conversation proved rich for both of us. When he learned that I was visiting the service center, he volunteered the information that he and his chief vestryman, the mayor, had just been talking about an expanded role for the church in assisting Haitian residents. That same day Charles came by to meet Marie, Bernard, and myself in Marie's house trailer office. Following introductions, our "guest" surprised us by requesting that we continue the meeting with prayer. It was clear from his words that he saw in our meeting a new opportunity for cooperative mission.[19].

I know little about the activities of church groups in the Mexican border communities of Texas, New Mexico, and Arizona, but I do have some acquaintance with efforts in San Diego County, where a growing Hispanic population that includes many illegal aliens has combined with large groups of refugees from southeast Asia to challenge old status quos. My guess is that ministries of hospitality similar to those in Florida are alive and well throughout the Southwest. Certainly the National Farm Worker Ministry, based in Salinas, California, has been doing productive work for years with migrant laborers. It will be important to monitor the progress of churches in this burgeoning sunbelt area as they attempt to form alliances among established citizens, newcomers from the east or midwest who are often seeking to escape multicultural problems, and strangers from other countries eager to share in the material prosperity of our land. Efforts along this line are now underway in New York City where an ecumenical ministry called "The Circus," focusing upon problems faced by Latin American immigrants, has created teams of theological students, social workers, and union organizers to join with the immigrants themselves in shaping their futures. Meanwhile, in Washington D.C., sensitive Christians are attempting to insure that legislation pertaining to the status of refugees and immigrants will approximate the hospitality urged by Jesus and the New Testament writers.[20] This is as it should be, for perhaps no other frontier today will prove so decisive for the configuration of American society in the next decade.

Applying themselves to this political task and to many other ministries of welcoming in Washington are the members of Luther Place Memorial Church, located just a few blocks northeast of the White House in the heart of the city's red-light district. In the early seventies this congregation began to define itself quite consciously as a center of urban hospitality. Having acquired a number of brownstone-type residential buildings in the immediate neighborhood, the people of Luther Place, under the leadership of their current pastor John Steinbruck, developed a village dedicated to meeting the critical needs of marginal people in the capital area. Presently this group of buildings, along with the sanctuary itself, offers an emergency night shelter, temporary dwellings for homeless men and women who are barely able to cope and/or work, a feeding program, a medical clinic, and living spaces for college students and seminarians who serve as volunteer workers. A significant amount of the food used in these operations is "gleaned" from Washington's many official receptions and banquets, as well as hotels.

High on the list of priorities for this congregation is the education of the church at large with regard to ministries of hospitality. Frequently youth groups and individuals from other parts of the country stay overnight to take part in the various projects. On the back page of the Sunday bulletin visitors attending worship are addressed as follows:

> The congregation of Luther Place believes itself to be guests in God's Creation and servants in and through this House and Village. . . . We welcome you to share the joyful responsibility of being faithful "innkeepers" who are called to make room for others. . . .[21]

Experimentation is the order of the day in this parish complex. A bakery is now in the works to provide bread for transients that will contain most of the basic nutrients in a day's ration. A weekend coffee house oriented toward prostitutes and other street people will soon be in operation.

During my last visit to Luther Place I took part in a well-attended "service of public sanctuary." At this event fifteen other religious groups joined the congregation in a Eucharist to welcome four Salvadoran refugees who had fled from the notorious "death squads" to enter the U.S. as illegal aliens. By housing the refugees and expressing public support for them, the welcomers were engaging in an act of civil disobedience designed to challenge current government policies. Later that night, as we talked, John Steinbruck told me about the rising spiritual and material costs of the ministry at Luther Place, but also about the exceptional generosity of those who had been touched by it, including a number of former "guests" and anonymous donors. His experience fits with the outcome of our exegetical work, which suggests that real hospitality not only serves guests but also feeds hosts and raises up partners. Just before I left, John pointed out some renovations in the sanctuary building. "Look," he said, "new doors. We're always wearing out our doors around here. Put that in your book!"

It could be argued that ministries like those at Luther Place derive largely from models worked out by nineteenth-century proponents of the Social Gospel. But it seems to me that they owe far more to the indomitable spirit of Dorothy Day and the Catholic Worker Movement that she helped to found. Following up on an idea from Peter

Maurin, Day and her other colleagues established "houses of hospitalit·" during the worst days of the Depression. These were far more than flophouses and soup kitchens. For one thing, the guests were barely distinguishable from the hosts, who lived very simple lives themselves. As we might expect, a number of role reversals took place. Day was fond of telling about those who thought they were just dropping in for a handout but ended up staying on for years as members of the staff. Moreover, Day insisted upon the primacy of the spiritual in all ministries of hospitality. At the center of efforts to meet the material needs of guests she expected a "painful dying to self" by guests and hosts alike that would be "rewarded by a tremendous increase of supernatural love."[22] Austere as she was, Day seems to have experienced God's abundance for the restoration of community.

Some would object that marginal organizations like the Catholic Worker Movement or the community of sisters headed by Mother Teresa of Calcutta can do little to alter the structures that make for poverty and despair in our time. That may be so, and yet the persistent attention given to these groups in the popular and church press indicates some kind of general fascination with the deeper dimensions of hospitality that they exemplify. This in itself could signal a readiness for fundamental changes.

In any event, there are ministries of hospitality committed to something more than the meeting of crisis-needs. One of these, now developing in Brooklyn, has been named "Project Nehemiah" in honor of the Israelite who returned from exile in Babylon to supervise the rebuilding of Jerusalem's walls. The project is sponsored by an ecumenical coalition of church groups, including the Roman Catholic Diocese of Brooklyn, which has pledged itself to raising twelve million dollars for the construction of five thousand single-family town houses in blighted areas of New York's most populous borough. Furthermore, the coalition has requested and received a commitment from the city government for an additional ten million dollars, as well as aid in converting abandoned sites to residential use. The hope is that these new homes will be purchased by lower-middle income people and that many neighborhoods will be restored. While formidable obstacles remain, Project Nehemiah seems destined for success. What strikes me as particularly noteworthy about it is that here the economic initiative was taken by a religious organization. As one city official put it, "No group has ever come to us like that before. Basically, they said, 'We've got our twelve million dollars; what have you got?' What else could we say?"[23]

Again and again, it seems, the grace of hospitality stimulates the creation of partnerships not generally thought to be possible. Other ministries devoted to long-term structural changes for marginal people are Millard Fuller's Habitat for Humanity, which carries on many of the ideals embodied at Clarence Jordan's Koinonia Farm,[24] and Bread for the World, a Christian citizens' group that seeks to help churches understand their role in alleviating world hunger, especially through political lobbying.[25] It will come as no surprise that the records of these organizations are filled with stories of sacrifice, abundance, and partnership with strangers.

Our topic in this section has been the discernment of frontiers for partnership. So far we have treated it as a matter of investigating current ministries of hospitality, with an eye toward generating or enhancing our own. But there is another sort of frontier, the first and last frontier really, because it discerns all the others. This is the frontier of the self, and this discerner must itself be examined. In her article "The Two Strangers" Ann Ulanov takes up the theme of alienation and shows from a psychological perspective how we treat others as foreigners or enemies to the extent that we withhold our welcome from parts of ourselves. Thus we project onto the outer stranger those features of our own psyches that we cannot accept because they threaten our "working" selfhood.[26] As long as we remain strangers to ourselves we cannot be good hosts in the world. The task then is to create a home within for these strangers, especially the deprived parts of our psyches whom we have neglected to feed and nurture.

The biblical term that best describes this task is repentance, that is, the renunciation of evil by means of a return to our true home with God. Jesus, Paul, and Luke all teach us that this is, at its core, a joyful journey. In the outer world it means finding reconciliation with neighbors or joining communities for whom generous sharing is a hallmark. In the inner world of the self it means experiencing peace (which is not necessarily the absence of conflict) among our warring factions. Perhaps no story in the New Testament exemplifies this *metanoia* better than the parable of the lost or prodigal son. Reduced by his dissolute life to the job of feeding unclean animals, the son experienced despair. But then—we are not told how—"he came to himself" and said, "How many of my father's hired servants have bread enough and to spare, but I perish here with hunger! I will arise and go to my father" (Luke 15:17–18). In an instant the son imagines himself, erring and needy, at the door of his father's house, where he knows he will be admitted. This is the core of repentance: to see ourselves before God as unworthy servants, but at the same time as guests and children of a Monarch who yearns for our company. Insofar as we envision ourselves this way (1 Cor. 11:31), we become capable of welcoming one another. In fact, when repentance takes on the character of a daily discipline, it becomes a basis for "natural" hospitality to strangers.

Writing about the inhabitants of the French village of Le Chambon, who saved thousands of Jews from the Nazis by sheltering them in their homes or guiding them across the border to Switzerland, Philip Hallie observes:

> I learned [from studying their story] that the opposite of cruelty is not simply freedom from the cruel relationship; it is *hospitality*. . . . When I asked them why they helped these dangerous guests, they invariably answered, "What do you mean, 'Why?' Where else could they go? How could you turn them away? What is so special about being ready to help *(prete a servir)?* There was nothing else to do." And some of them laughed in amazement when I told them I thought they were "good people."[27]

But they *were* nevertheless good people, precisely because they acted so consistently out of their own characters. In wondering about the motivation for their remarkable behavior, Hallie offers two explanations. First, the Chambonnais were Huguenots, marginal people in Catholic France who knew from their heritage the terror of being hunted to the death. Thus, they were able to "feel with" the Jewish refugees they welcomed. Second, their leaders, particularly their pastor André Trocmé, kept reminding them that "every human being was like Jesus, had God in him or her, and was just as precious as God himself."[28] For these villagers, repentance in the sense of a return to their fullest selves before God was simply a way of life.

Today we need this repentance very badly if we are going to sustain human connections with those who are usually perceived as our enemies. Clearly the cause of world peace is advanced by programs designed to encourage personal visits and letters between ourselves and the people of the U.S.S.R. Among the most intriguing of these is the Pairing Project founded by Earl Molander, a professor of business management at Portland State University. Molander's project, based on the sister city concept, has helped to develop sharing links between eight hundred American communities, mostly small towns and medium-sized cities, and equivalent municipalities in the Soviet Union. Typically, packets of information containing material from such local groups as the chamber of commerce, scouts, League of Women Voters, hockey team, and so on are sent to the Soviet partners. When similar packets are received, personal relationships between individuals and exchanges of letters often follow.[29] Whether or not this program is motivated by overtly religious concerns, it serves to illustrate the transcendence of hostility that always accompanies joyful repentance. The repentant self comes to know the congruity between its inner frontiers and the international situation. The self in homecoming grasps the promise and mission of partnership with strangers.

THE ABIDING MYSTERY OF GOD'S WELCOME

So there are many frontiers of hospitality, some inside us, some outside, some pleasant and nourishing, some perilous. But there is One who turns them all into welcomes and is revealed through them. The pilgrim people of Israel knew this well, for one of their number wrote:

> The Lord is my shepherd, I shall not want;
> he makes me lie down in green pastures.
> He leads me beside still waters;
> he restores my soul. . . .
>
> Thou preparest a table in the presence of my enemies,
> thou anointest my head with oil,
>   my cup overflows.
> Surely goodness and mercy shall follow me all the days of
>   my life;
> and I shall dwell in the house of the Lord for ever.
>
> (Psalm 23)

I wonder if Jesus did not have this psalm in mind when he urged his followers to petition God for the coming of the kingdom, for the bread of tomorrow today. Certainly the Lord's Prayer is like Psalm 23 in the expectation of its author that God will provide nurture and refuge in the midst of troubled times.

The times remain troubled, down to this present day. And we remain pilgrims, like the psalmist and the disciples of Jesus. However strong our faith, however skilled we become in the roles of guest and host, we are wanderers still. At some very deep level we are still "lost in the cosmos," to use Walker Percy's painful phrase.[30] But we are also searched for and known and met. Indeed, the mystery of God's welcome is that it so frequently encounters us when we most need to be, but cannot allow ourselves to be, guests.

Often, we discover, this welcome comes to us through strangers, and not infrequently in the course of our service to them. Philip Potter of the World Council of Churches reminds us that in Christ we learn to receive gifts from those who approach us with empty hands. But this requires the continuing conversion of repentance. Sometimes our "angels" will not be those who come to us for help but simply the remarkable people we meet in everyday life. To receive the welcomes borne by these messengers we need to trust that God is always at work sanctifying the ordinary, turning even tedious situations into homecomings. Parker Palmer alludes to this common grace of hospitality when he writes:

> The stranger of public life becomes the spiritual guide of our private life. Through the stranger our view of self, of world, of God is deepened and expanded. Through the stranger we are given a chance to find ourselves. And through the stranger, God finds us and offers us the gift of wholeness in the midst of our estranged lives.[31]

The kingdom of God is a persistent invitation to Being which seeks us out in the fortresses of our alienation.

The kingdom is also a great feast which spreads itself in our hearts and deeds. A friend of long standing, Sister Marilyn Robinson, recently commemorated twenty-five years of service in the Order of St. Ursula, some of it as an itinerant teacher and liturgist in the Ozarks. Because we have often talked about hospitality, she knew I would want to reflect on a parable she had written to celebrate her quarter-century of ministry. In many ways, I think, it offers us a cameo portrait of New Testament hospitality:

> The Kingdom of God is like a seed planted in a woman's heart
>> slowly, silently stretching it
>> beyond family and friends, church and nation
>> until one day that heart bursts open
>> revealing a Table
>>> wider than the world
>>> warm as an intimate embrace.
>
> To this Table everyone is invited
>> no one is stranger, no one unfit;
>> each brings a gift, work of one's own hands, heart,
>>> mind
>> —a morsel for the Table—
> and there is always enough
>> enough because no one keeps hidden the
>>> bread of the morrow
>> enough because in the sharing is the
>>> miracle of multiplication.
>
> Around this Table everyone eats
>> and no one is stuffed;
>> each sips deeply of love unearned
>> and offers the cup to another.
>
> From this Table each rises
>> strengthened by a morsel and a sip
>> heart seeded
>> pregnant.[32]

Thus the kingdom perpetuates itself by growing up in its guests and coming to birth in their ministry as hosts.

Yet the guest role never really ceases. It is sometimes thought that George Herbert composed the poem now called "Love III" as he contemplated the Eucharist in his tiny church at Bemerton near Salisbury. Whatever its origin, his work stands as one of the most eloquent testimonies ever given to the power of God's hospitality:

> Love bade me welcome; yet my soul drew back,
>> Guiltie of dust and sinne.
> But quick-ey'd Love, observing me grow slack
>> From my first entrance in,
> Drew nearer to me, sweetly questioning,
>> If I lack'd any thing.
>
> 'A guest,' I answer'd, 'worthy to be here':
>> Love said, 'You shall be he.'

'I the unkinde, ungratefull? Ah my deare,
    I cannot look on Thee.'
Love took my hand, and smiling did reply,
    'Who made the eyes but I?'

'Truth Lord, but I have marr'd them; let my shame
    Go where it doth deserve.'
'And know you not,' sayes Love, 'Who bore the blame?'
    'My deare, then I will serve.'
'You must sit down,' sayes Love, 'and taste My meat.'
    So I did sit and eat.[33]

Busy, unworthy servants like ourselves will always find it hard to sit and eat, to taste and see that the Lord is good. But this is the great and first commandment of New Testament hospitality. If we take it to heart, we shall do well.

NOTES

1. Nouwen, *Reaching Out,* 50–54.
2. *NYT,* 26 Aug. 1981, sec. C, 1, 8.
3. I refer to the mutual prophesying and upbuilding that Paul considered to be a regular feature of the church's worship. See 1 Corinthians 14, esp. vv. 20–25.
4. Wilfred Bockelman's newsletter is published from 1207 N.E. Constance Blvd., Ham Lake, MN 55303.
5. Palmer, *Company of Strangers,* 131.
6. Ibid., 132.
7. Nouwen, *Reaching Out,* 56–63.
8. Elizabeth O'Conner, *The New Community: A Portrait of Life Together in Words and Pictures* (New York: Harper & Row, 1976), 53.
9. See chap. 2, n. 58, on the reconstruction of the Lord's Prayer by Jeremias used here.
10. Russell, *Growth in Partnership,* 15–38, esp. 33.
11. Michael Walzer, *Spheres of Justice: A Defense of Pluralism and Equality* (New York: Basic Books, 1983), 316–18.
12. Ibid., 318.
13. Ibid., 59.
14. Ibid., 60.
15. O'Conner, *New Community,* 21.
16. The phrase comes from Matthew Lamb's *Solidarity with Victims: Toward a Theology of Social Transformation* (New York: Crossroad, 1982). Lamb does not wish to deny the mutuality involved in this solidarity (see the

preface to his book), but his ruling image strikes me as unnecessarily static and open to romantic interpretations.

17. Paul Moore, Jr., and John H. Burt, "It's Time to Explore Industrial Policies That Aid Communities," NYT, 9 Sept. 1982, editorial page.

18. NYT, 12 Nov. 1984: A1, B11.

19. At this writing (summer 1984) the ministry in Belle Glade continues to proceed with vigor. A Head Start program for children and a credit union for adults are scheduled to open in the fall.

20. It is becoming clear that the immigration bill still pending in Congress at this writing would solve only a few problems and probably create more. Legislators representing Hispanic-Americans tend to regard the bill as unjust.

21. Bulletin for 20 March 1983.

22. Dorothy Day in The Catholic Worker (January–February 1982):3 (from a letter by her first published in January, 1948). See also Dorothy Day's Loaves and Fishes (New York: Curtis Books, 1963), 28–41.

23. NYT, 30 July 1982: sec. B, 7.

24. Millard Fuller and Diane Scott, Love in the Mortar Joints: The Story of Habitat for Humanity (Piscataway, N.J.: New Century Publishers, 1980).

25. See, e.g., the newsletter and reports published from Bread for the World's headquarters at 802 Rhode Island Ave, N.E., Washington D.C. 20018.

26. Ann Ulanov, "The Two Strangers," USQR 4 (1973): 273–83.

27. Philip Hallie, "From Cruelty to Goodness," The Hastings Center Report 11 (1981): 26–27. A more extensive documentation of the relevant events appears in Hallie's Lest Innocent Blood Be Shed: The Story of the Village of Le Chambon and How Goodness Happened There (San Francisco: Harper & Row, 1980).

28. Hallie, "From Cruelty to Goodness," 27.

29. NYT, 25 Nov. 1983: sec. A, 25.

30. See Walker Percy, Lost in the Cosmos: The Last Self-Help Book (New York: Farrar, Straus & Giroux, 1983).

31. Palmer, Company of Strangers, 70.

32. From personal correspondence dated 28 Nov. 1983.

33. The Oxford Book of Christian Verse, ed. David Cecil (Oxford: At the Clarendon Press, 1951), 136–137.

Suggestions
for Further Reading

Bellah, Robert, Richard Madsen, William Sullivan, Ann Swidler, and Stephen Tipton. *Habits of the Heart: Individualism and Commitment in American Life*. Berkeley and Los Angeles: Univ. of Calif. Press, 1985. Through depiction of representative men and women this study probes the tension between individualism and public commitment in American life.

Dillon, Richard J. *From Eye-Witnesses to Ministers of the Word: Tradition and Composition in Luke 24*. Rome: Biblical Institute Press, 1978. A closely-argued exegetical study which presents valuable hypotheses regarding Luke's itinerant predecessors.

Elliott, John H. *A Home for the Homeless: A Sociological Exegesis of 1 Peter, Its Situation and Strategy*. Philadelphia: Fortress Press, 1981. A prime example of the new sociological approach to New Testament studies. Includes considerable information about the practice of hospitality in early Christian households.

Jeremias, Joachim. *The Eucharistic Words of Jesus*. Translated by N. Perrin. New York: Charles Scribner's Sons, 1966. A classic treatment of the last supper, especially the words of institution, within the context of Jesus' whole ministry. Deserves a new reading by modern exegetes.

Jewett, Robert J. *Christian Tolerance: Paul's Message to the Modern Church*. Biblical Perspectives on Current Issues. Philadelphia: Westminster Press, 1982. An exegetical-systematic study of mutual acceptance and welcoming in the churches established through Paul's mission. Centers upon material from Romans.

Johnson, Luke T. *Sharing Possessions: Mandate and Symbol of Faith*. Overtures to Biblical Theology. Philadelphia: Fortress Press, 1981. Investigates the economic dimensions of Christian community life. Contrasts New Testament views on renouncing wealth and almsgiving and presents a contemporary argument for the latter.

Malherbe, Abraham J. *Social Aspects of Early Christianity*. 2d ed. Philadelphia: Fortress Press, 1983. Contains two essays of special relevance for our topic: "House Churches and Their Problems" and "Hospitality and Inhospitality in the Church."

Meeks, Wayne A. *The First Urban Christians: The Social World of the Apostle Paul.* New Haven: Yale Univ. Press, 1983. A thematic approach to Pauline Christianity as a socioeconomic phenomenon of the Greco-Roman world. Stresses the "welcoming" character of the Pauline communities.

Nouwen, Henri J. M. *Reaching Out: The Three Movements of the Spiritual Life.* New York: Doubleday & Co., 1975. A pastoral essay in which the second movement treated is entitled "From Hostility to Hospitality." An early stimulus to my own work.

Palmer, Parker J. *The Company of Strangers: Christians and the Renewal of America's Public Life.* New York: Crossroad, 1981. Contains illuminating discussions of "Life among Strangers" and "The Stranger as Spiritual Guide" within contemporary society.

Perrin, Norman. *Rediscovering the Teaching of Jesus.* New York: Harper & Row, 1967. Expands upon earlier work by Joachim Jeremias in understanding Jesus' table fellowship with outcasts as a central aspect of his kingdom proclamation.

Russell, Letty M. *Growth in Partnership.* Philadelphia: Westminster Press, 1981. A practical-theological approach to human partnership with God in the New Creation; argues for a form of liberation theology.

Sampley, J. Paul. *Pauline Partnership in Christ: Christian Community and Commitment in Light of Roman Law.* Philadelphia: Fortress Press, 1980. Shows the creative interaction between Paul's experience of Christ in community and the Roman notion of *societas;* focuses primarily upon Philippians, Philemon, and the Corinthian correspondence.

Schüssler Fiorenza, Elisabeth. *In Memory of Her: A Feminist Theological Reconstruction of Christian Origins.* New York: Crossroad, 1983. Presents fruitful hypotheses regarding the structures of authority in the Jesus movement, the early Christian missionary effort, and the residential churches reflected in our New Testament documents.

Theissen, Gerd. *Sociology of Early Palestinian Christianity.* Translated by J. Bowden. Philadelphia: Fortress Press, 1978. A ground-breaking study of the interaction between two types of early Christians: "wandering charismatics" and urban residents. Socioeconomic and theological factors are explored.

Verhey, Alan. *The Great Reversal: Ethics and the New Testament.* Grand Rapids: Wm. B. Eerdmans, 1984. An exegetical-theological treatment of Christian ethics in which the appropriate human response to Jesus' message is understood to be "welcoming the kingdom."

Walzer, Michael. *Spheres of Justice: A Defense of Pluralism and Equality.* New York: Basic Books, 1983. An approach to distributive justice by a social philosopher; membership in a community is found to be the foundational good from which "complex equality" can be derived.

Index

151

156   *INDEX*

OTHER JEWISH AND
CHRISTIAN LITERATURE